"In this book Darryl Stephens not only
of Exodus to the realities that many churc......
ing and affirming,' but he also inspires congregations that choose to take
this journey through what can be a traumatic transition."

—Tony Campolo
Eastern University

"The biblical story of Exodus is one of movement: from Egypt to Sinai,
from slavery under Pharaoh to relationship with God, and from degrading
oppression to true freedom. This volume wonderfully works and unpacks
these texts to show how we ourselves can move: from hardness of heart to
compassion, from rigid ways of thinking to openness of heart and mind,
from exclusion to invitation . . . and eventually onward to respect and love.
It should be on every Christian's bookshelf, both those who are working
for full inclusion and those who are struggling along the way. A wonderful
resource for the church!"

—Roy L. Heller
Associate Professor, Perkins School of Theology

"This is such an important work. In *Out of Exodus*, Stephens challenges
our narrow notions of what the Bible teaches about our LGBTQIA+ family. He reminds us that we are all precious, anointed, and beloved children
created in the image of the Divine. This book teaches us that we are all on
the journey together and that we must stay in this struggle together, in the
name of God."

—M. Garlinda Burton
Executive Director, Nashville Freedom School Partnership

"*Out of Exodus* is an engaging spiritual journey about Christians seeking to be in ministry with people of diverse sexual orientations and perspectives. Darryl Stephens, a person of deep faith and scholarly intellect, has written a book that includes Biblical groundings, pastoral reflections and personal stories . . . As a pastor who has been engaged in this journey for over 40 years, I believe *Out of Exodus* will be a helpful tool for assisting churches in their desire to be in ministry with people of diverse sexual orientations."

—Jim Bankston
Retired Clergy, St. Paul's United Methodist Church, Houston, Texas

"*Out of Exodus* offers poignant insight into the various perspectives of those with whom we worship. These personal stories offer opportunities for the reader's self-reflection, and I would recommend this work to those wishing to explore issues of faith and inclusion within the congregation of believers."

—Michelle Daniels
Christ Servant Minister, The United Methodist Church

"In a time when entire denominations are threatening to split over human sexuality issues, Darryl Stephens in *Out of Exodus* offers us the account of a refreshing journey taken by a congregation in south-central Pennsylvania to face challenging moral issues and find God's grace in the midst of faithful wrestling and societal ambiguity. . . . The hope of finding and preserving the church's unity in the face of moral ambiguity and uncertainty for many shines through the testimony of this volume. It should be an encouraging and helpful resource to many."

—Bruce C. Birch
Dean, Wesley Theological Seminary

"It was so, so good for us! The sharing was amazing. We are moving forward. The best part of studying *Out of Exodus* for us was how it solicited sharing. We felt safe and it opened up our hearts."

—Jonette Gay
Pastor, Otterbein United Methodist Church

"Combining Scripture, sermons, dialogue, and lived experiences, *Out of Exodus* is a phenomenal resource for any spiritual community interested in expanding their welcome to all God's people—especially those interested in the Reconciling process."

—M. Barclay
Reconciling Ministries Network

"What a refreshing perspective. A sort of victory as opposed to just an apologetic. Rather than pick apart 'the gay clobber passages,' Stephens views the journey through multiple lenses: the heart of God for bringing people out of captivity, the history of the church in that trek, the experiences of individual believers in their walk, and the position we can reasonably embrace in the light of that odyssey. I love the book. There are so many people I hope will read it!"

—Marsha Stevens-Pino
Author of *For Those Tears I Died*

"*Out of Exodus* is a unique book that allows the reader to journey with a congregation as it becomes open and affirming of LGBTQIA+ people. The book is structured around the Exodus story and provides sermons, reflections, testimonies, and quotes from clergy and members of the congregation. Readers learn how clergy and lay leaders helped to guide conversation and reflection, how members came to new conclusions, and how genuine engagement with Scripture, tradition, reason, and experience led to spiritual growth."

—Marie Alford-Harkey
President and CEO, Religious Institute

OUT OF EXODUS

OUT OF EXODUS

A Journey of Open and Affirming Ministry

by
Darryl W. Stephens
with
Michael I. Alleman,
Andrea Brown,
Ruth A. Daugherty,
and **Mary Merriman**

Foreword by
John C. Holbert

CASCADE *Books* · Eugene, Oregon

OUT OF EXODUS
A Journey of Open and Affirming Ministry

Cascade Books
An Imprint of Wipf and Stock Publishers
199 W. 8th Ave., Suite 3
Eugene, OR 97401

www.wipfandstock.com

PAPERBACK ISBN: 978-1-5326-3028-6
HARDCOVER ISBN: 978-1-5326-3030-9
EBOOK ISBN: 978-1-5326-3029-3

Cataloguing-in-Publication data:

Names: Stephens, Darryl W., author | Alleman, Michael I., author. | Brown, Andrea, author. | Daugherty, Ruth A., author. | Merriman, Mary, author. | Holbert, John C., foreword.

Title: Book title : Out of exodus : a journey of open and affirming ministry / Darryl W. Stephens with Michael I. Alleman, Andrea Brown, Ruth A. Daugherty, and Mary Merriman ; foreword by John C. Holbert.

Description: Eugene, OR : Cascade Books, 2018 | Includes bibliographical references.

Identifiers: ISBN 978-1-5326-3028-6 (paperback) | ISBN 978-1-5326-3030-9 (hardcover) | ISBN 978-1-5326-3029-3 (ebook)

Subjects: LCSH: United Methodist Church (U.S.)—Doctrines. | Church controversies—United States—Case studies. | Sex—Religious aspects—United Methodist Church. | Homosexuality—Religious aspects—Christianity. | Gender identity—Religious aspects—Christianity. | Identity (Psychology)—Religious aspects—Christianity.

Classification: BX8332 .S74 2018 (paperback) | BX8332 .S74 (ebook)

Manufactured in the U.S.A.   04/24/18

Genderbread Person v3.3 by Sam Killermann. Used by permission.

Lyrics of "For Those Tears I Died" copyright © 1969 Bud John Songs (ASCAP) (adm. at CapitolCMGPublishing.com) All rights reserved. Used by permission.

"Ten Ideas for Breaking the Silence Around Sexuality" provided by and reprinted with permission of Drew Konow, Director of Communications and LGBTQ Programs at the Religious Institute.

Scripture quotations are from the New Revised Standard Version, copyright © 1989 by the Division of Christian Education of the National Council of the Churches of Christ in the United States of America.

This book is dedicated to the people of Grandview United Methodist Church and all persons intent on "making gentle a bruised world."

Contents

Act V: **Setting Out on a New Journey** | 123

Foreword

I was ordained a Deacon in the North Texas Conference of The United Methodist Church in 1970, in the time when full ordination was a two-step process, the final step being the move to Elder, which happened for me in the Louisiana Conference in 1976. I then spent the remainder of my ministry, a primarily academic one, in the Central Texas Conference, teaching first at Texas Wesleyan College (now University) and lastly at Perkins School of Theology until my retirement, after thirty-three years in that place, in 2012. During my teaching ministry, I was blessed to have preached and taught in over 1000 churches in forty states and twenty countries. I thank God each day for the grand privilege of my fulfilling and enriching ministry during those active years.

However, through all that time there has always been one particularly dark stain on my denomination, one that persists, appallingly and shockingly, up to the time of this writing in 2017. That blot is the exclusion of my LGBTQ sisters and brothers from full involvement in the life of this church: no recognized ordination and no official right to perform same-sex weddings, whether the one who officiates is gay or straight. All of this has occurred amid near-constant overt and covert slanders and bickering among clergy and laypersons wielding Bible verses as clubs and displaying the most egregious forms of hypocrisy imaginable. The well-trammeled United Methodist slogan, "Open hearts, open minds, open doors," is regularly and often shamelessly bruited about with no recognition that it is false on its face. And all this despite continuous attempts to undo this church's stance, ensconced in its *Book of Discipline* since 1972, that homosexuality is "incompatible with Christian teaching." It remains very painful to me that nearly all of my days as a minister of The United Methodist Church have been overshadowed by this reality.

In more than a few of my preaching and teaching opportunities in churches, I have tried to make it as plain as I can that the usual reasons given for this exclusion, especially the biblical ones, are, in effect, not valid. As others have made much clearer and more forcefully than I, the verses often employed to assault homosexual and transgender persons simply have been misread and thus misused as weapons against a whole group of people, many of whom have heard a distinct call from God for all sorts of Christian service. I cannot number the students I have had over the years who have had to make the agonizing choice of whether to remain in the closet—and thus deny their true selves in order to become ministers in our church—or to find a denomination that will celebrate their gifts and receive them gladly and fully into their ministry. United Methodism has lost countless servants in this way. One can only weep at the loss and rejoice as these persons find ways to live out their callings elsewhere.

Darryl Stephens's book is a welcome disruption of this painful reality. It offers to us a much-needed statement of one congregation's story as it moved toward becoming a Reconciling Congregation (one fully accepting of LGBTQ persons, in United Methodist lingo, at least as far as the restrictive language of the *Discipline* will allow) and the many persons and experiences that made that journey possible. Grandview UMC in Lancaster, Pennsylvania, is that church—and a grand view it has indeed.

Stephens does an excellent job of modeling for us just how a church can become inclusive by offering in his pages the voices of multiple members of the congregation, both gay and straight—from a well-known leader and crusader in Methodism, to a former clergy member of the Metropolitan Community Church (now a staff person at Grandview), to several church members from various locations on the spectrum of an obviously diverse church community. Stephens gives these voices a full-throated role in the church's struggle toward a public statement of inclusivity for all. In that way, the church's inclusiveness is witnessed in the very diverse pages of this book.

As I read the book, a title of another volume I read long ago kept intruding into my thoughts. In 1976, Herbert Schneidau wrote *Sacred Discontent*, a perceptive analysis of the Bible that claimed that an honest appraisal of the old book should lead a reader to look very hard at all received knowledge and be ready to have it challenged in order to make it possible to hear something genuinely new. Stephens uses the phrase "holy disruption" perhaps in the same way. In the matter of human sexuality, all of us need such a holy disruption. We must be afflicted with a sacred discontent if we are ever to open ourselves up to the new and complex sexual world in which we all live. The old binary claim of "either man or woman" will no longer suffice as an adequate description of who we are as sexual beings. We all desperately need to learn what the Bible, science, and our own experiences are teaching us about our human family.

This book is not so much a reasoned argument as it is a complex piece of visual evidence for this new world. Stephens asks us to hear the disparate voices, to listen with care to real people who live and apprehend the world in ways different from those who have too long assumed that the "received wisdom" is the only wisdom there may be.

Some years ago, a beloved former colleague of mine, Dr. Joe Allen, in an address that marked his forty-two years of teaching ethics on the faculty of Perkins School of Theology, said something like the following: "If it is true that same-sex orientation is not a learned experience but an innate one, then to be gay is little different than being left-handed. As such, it cannot be the subject of ethical debate beyond the usual discussion of appropriate and inappropriate sexual behavior between human beings. Same-sex behavior cannot be deemed right or wrong in and of itself any more than left or right handedness can be." Thus, it must be said that United Methodism is quite wrong about this matter and has been officially quite wrong for forty-five years. Darryl Stephens's book is a gift to those of us who know that is true and who hope beyond hope that a new day is dawning, a day that will see the full inclusion of our LGBTQ colleagues at all levels of our mission and ministry in every denomination.

John C. Holbert
Lois Craddock Perkins Professor of Homiletics Emeritus
Perkins School of Theology
June 20, 2017

Preface

This book is not what you think it is. Whether conservative or liberal, evangelical or mainline, young or old, traditionalist or progressive, your expectations will likely be upended. Personal testimony and faith sharing, practices accepted and even expected among evangelicals and conservative Christians, raise red flags of warning for moderate and progressive mainline Christians. We've too often been accosted by would-be proselytizers trying to make their own experience of salvation fit everyone else. The language of sexual orientation and gender identity likewise raises signals of alert for conservative and many evangelical Christians. We've too often met folks whose "faith" has no discernable impact on how they live their lives day to day, and these phrases evoke a cultural and moral relativism at odds with our understanding of holy living. This book dares to bridge these divides.

Out of Exodus is an affirmation that we can be both biblical and progressive in our faith. Personal testimonies by pastors, lay leaders, parents, and family members stand in parallel with the story of Exodus, the journey of the ancient Israelites learning what it means to be the people of God. Both communities experienced plagues, trials, dangerous crossings, and wandering through the wilderness. The stories in this book include experiences of and with persons in many denominational settings: Roman Catholic, Unitarian-Universalist, Presbyterian Church in Taiwan, Metropolitan Community Church, United Church of Christ, United Brethren, Church of the Brethren, Society of Friends (Quakers), and United Methodist. This is truly an ecumenical journey.

This book is meant to help us learn to be the people of God in the social wilderness of today. Many families, individuals, and congregations are struggling to discern God's will in these times of intense social change, particularly with regard to how to be in ministry with persons of diverse sexual orientations and gender identities. Among moderate to progressive churches and their members, there is a great need for biblically-based, fully-inclusive sermons, innovative Bible study materials, and truthful stories of being in ministry with all persons. Christians are hungry for spiritual encounters that encourage our questions, spark debate, nurture our souls, and inspire our hearts. Let there be no doubt: the Spirit is strong. God is still speaking.

Out of Exodus is the testimony of a community of faith discerning how to be open and affirming in ministry. Grandview United Methodist Church is situated in Lancaster, Pennsylvania, in an affluent suburb of a small city in a county that consistently votes Republican within a state that still permits employers to fire persons and landlords to deny housing to people because they are gay or lesbian. This congregation is also situated within a denomination terribly divided by differing views on homosexuality. Yet, from the land of shoofly pie, scrapple, and Amish farms arises a Holy-Spirit-led ministry of radical hospitality and inclusion.

In this book, you will find stories of faith. You will read personal testimonies about what it means to be homosexual and Christian. You will encounter sermons that wrestle with what it means to be open and affirming in ministry. You will read the Bible as a story of faith in which we ourselves find a place. You may even experience the presence of the Holy Spirit, especially if you study this book in the company of other Christians seeking to find God in our midst. If you are seeking the guidance of the Holy Spirit, encouragement from fellow Christians, and spiritual nourishment for the journey, this book is for you.

Hearing the individual testimonies shared at Grandview, I am convinced that there is an integral connection between God's concern for the immigrant (Exodus 22:21)—God's preferential option and special protection—and our ministry with lesbian, gay, bisexual, transgender, questioning, queer,[1] intersexual, androgynous, and asexual (LGBTQIA+) persons. The story of Exodus reminds us that we were once aliens in a hostile land. The word "alien" can mean immigrant, sojourner, or foreigner. It can also mean strange or unfamiliar—queer, even. In this journey of open and affirming ministry, we may find ourselves encountering persons who seem alien—even as we remember that we are all alien in some way or other. In

---

1. The word "queer" can be jarring to the ears of folks who have heard this as a derogatory term. In recent years, though, the word has been reclaimed by scholars and activists as a positive and provocative descriptor. See glossary in the appendices.

this encounter, I hear an echo of God's command to the Israelites (Exodus 23:9). We are all equally recipients of Christ's promise: "I came that they may have life, and have it abundantly" (John 10:10b).

This book is a witness to the journey that brought this congregation to a place of open and affirming ministry. In the spring of 2014, Grandview UMC voted to join the Reconciling Ministries Network (RMN).

> Reconciling Ministries Network envisions a renewed and vibrant Wesleyan movement that is biblically and theologically centered. As committed disciples of Jesus Christ, the Reconciling Ministries Network strives to transform the world by living out the Gospel's teachings of grace, love, justice and inclusion for all of God's children.[2]

Of course, Methodists are not unique in this ministry. There are similar organizations in many mainline denominations. Variously labeled "reconciling," "welcoming," "more light," or "open and affirming," thousands of mainline congregations have risked radical hospitality as a response to God's missional call to love and justice in the world.

Embarking on this journey with the people of Grandview has taught me that an open and affirming ministry is about much more than sexual orientation or gender identity. When I asked one member about the congregation's recent vote to become open and affirming, Carolyn replied that the congregation has always been open and affirming. She then proceeded to tell me about the numerous refugee families the congregation has sponsored over the decades. For her, providing hospitality to the immigrant in our midst is central to what it means to be God's people. We are both citizen and immigrant, each of us. Through Carolyn's testimony and the testimonies of others, I continue to learn anew what the Lord requires: "to do justice, and to love kindness, and to walk humbly with your God" (Micah 6:8). This humble walk is the journey of our faith.

Each Christian, each local church, and every manifestation of the Body of Christ must travel its own journey of faith. Each must take on and live into its new identity. This book shares the story of one congregation encountering the challenge of how to include the excluded, how to embrace the ostracized, and how to offer welcome to persons who have experienced the opposite—even and especially from Christian communities. While the testimonies here focus mainly on this congregation's growth in ministry with LGBTQIA+ persons, this experience has challenged Grandview to

2. RMN, "Vision."

consider how to be welcoming of many others. Becoming open and affirming of persons of diverse sexual orientation and gender identity has prepared us for meeting further challenges. For example, this predominantly white congregation is now engaged in discussions about white privilege, overcoming racism, and furthering our work with refugee families. The journey of becoming truly welcoming is the ongoing journey of faith.

I hope that this book inspires you and your congregation to claim this journey—and the Good News offered in the Bible—for yourself and to share your testimony with each other and with persons you meet everyday. You can begin wherever you find yourself, gaining inspiration and courage to address the human struggles in your midst. Each and every one of us is entrusted with the message of reconciliation (2 Corinthians 5:19). I firmly believe that God is doing a new thing in our midst and will continue to do so for all who are open to the movement of the Holy Spirit, offering us the gift of radically inclusive love (*agape*). Open and affirming ministry requires, in the language of The United Methodist Church (UMC), "Open hearts. Open minds. Open doors." May we continue to live into this declaration. May God the Father, Son, and Holy Spirit, Mother of us all, be with you now and forever!

TESTIMONY BY MARY MERRIMAN

Early on, while learning to love my sisters and brothers of Grandview UMC, I began to hear the stories of parents who had raised their sons and daughters in the church, as faithful followers would do. Nearly half a century ago, The United Methodist Church officially declared their doors closed to the gay and lesbian children whom they had raised in the Methodist faith, and it has broken many parents' hearts.[3] I understand their pain.

In 1976, I was a student leader at Montgomery Junior College in Takoma Park, Maryland. At twenty-five, I was considered an older student, as were many of us going to school on the GI bill. In 1973, homosexuality was removed from the list of mental disorders and a conversation about equality was beginning on college campuses. A new student club was formed on our campus to advocate for the concerns of lesbian and gay people. Two

---

3. In 1972, The United Methodist Church declared, "we do not condone the practice of homosexuality and consider this practice incompatible with Christian teaching." UMC, *The Book of Discipline 1972*, 86. This statement in the Social Principles remained virtually unchanged, as of 2018.

friends were staffing the table. As we talked, they indicated a need for a break and I offered to sit at the table. I was not "out" publicly until about fifteen minutes later when another student came up to the table where I was sitting and asked if I was a homosexual. At that moment, I made a choice to disclose one of the most intimate details of my life, one that could potentially have serious repercussions for my future (which it did!).

Homosexuality was not decriminalized in the U.S. at that time, and penalties differed from state to state. The religious right was ramping up their campaign of terror. People were living in isolation and fear of losing the support of families, churches, employment, and housing. However, while the decision to come out can have a wide range of negative effects, those effects can also be positive. The conspiracy of silence is broken. People have the ability to create links of support in community, churches, and families who are willing to extend their hands of love. God's love and blessing is not compromised from the pulpit, in the pews, or on the streets!

My testimony is from the perspective of a clergy and civil rights leader. Each LGBTQIA+ person has their own experiences of heartbreak as well as triumph. There has been a lot of drama played out over the past forty years in the quest for human rights for LGBTQIA+ persons. At times, I'm overwhelmed with emotions like anger regarding the abuse of LGBTQIA+ Christians by religious extremists as well as by once-caring and bold faith partners of our former church homes. I'm also anxious and feel helpless at times, seeking civil liberties at the state and federal level to protect LGBTQIA+ persons from discrimination in housing, employment, public accommodations, and education. As we journey with LGBTQIA+ persons in our congregations, each of us must be sensitive to God's Spirit, seeking ways to bring healing and hope to restore the brokenness that has occurred. As congregations open their doors, I urge them to invite LGBTQIA+ persons to share their stories as they feel led.

While reaching out to LGBTQIA+ people is important, so too is preparing a space in the hearts of a congregation. Discernment requires that everyone within a congregation has opportunity to examine their own conviction, beliefs, attitudes, and barriers that have separated and isolated many people of God from LGBTQIA+ persons, many of whom also share Christian faith. I began sharing my own beliefs with Grandview's pastors, the congregation's Reconciling Ministry Team, and the adult Searchers Class. I preached sermons, wrote in the newsletter, participated in Bible studies, and engaged in other forms of faith sharing. Grandview's pastors explored the story of Exodus in a series of sermons, which provided stimulating conversation and prompted an exploration of racism, heterosexism, homophobia, and oppression. This book includes those sermons and reflections, in the hope that they will stimulate similar conversations in your faith community.

Acknowledgments

Every book is, in some way, a collective effort. This book is especially so. Many people at Grandview UMC and beyond contributed their time and talents to create and improve *Out of Exodus*. Authorship is noted throughout this book, and unattributed portions are my own.

I would like to express my heartfelt appreciation to pastors Michael Alleman and Andrea Brown. The fruit of their prophetic leadership at Grandview UMC over many years is apparent in numerous personal testimonies and the decision of this faith community to become a Reconciling Congregation in March 2014. I am especially grateful for their sermon series on Exodus from June 14 to August 31, 2014, which prompted me to imagine this book. This wisp of a thought would have evaporated had not Kirstin Shrom-Rhoads, then a student-pastor at Grandview, prompted me a few months later to consider my own spiritual gifts in the ministry of Grandview UMC. In her wisdom, she asked open-ended questions and encouraged me to act on this vision. Thank you, Kirstin.

The book then became the work of the community. I would like to express my tremendous gratitude to both Ruth Daugherty, for her leadership at Grandview and throughout the UMC and for sharing her personal reflections in response to each sermon, and Mary Merriman, not only for her career in ministry on the frontlines of justice but also for sharing her testimony in these pages. Andrea Brown offers the following acknowledgement in the context of her sermon "Responsibility / Refuge":

> Mary has written a detailed, factual account of the events that are recounted in this sermon, based on my recollection of several conversations with her about these events. As pastors tend to do in crafting a sermon, I have taken a small amount of license in my retelling—but not much. I greatly admire the courage of pioneers such as Mary and the Rev. Troy Perry, who, despite

life-threatening, soul-tearing circumstances, helped to bring the church and the nation forward in our understanding of sexuality and Christianity.

Mary is a grace-filled pioneer who has helped us become the open and affirming congregation that we are today.

Thank you to members of Grandview who responded to my invitation to "be the book" through a sharing and listening session, via email, and through personal interviews: Marge and Lou Cumpston, Connie Brown, Dorothy Killebrew, Carolyn Kendall, Emma Lou Kraft, Carolene Brubaker, Jessica Kahler, and others. Thank you also to Liz Fulmer for transcribing Michael Alleman's sermons.

I am grateful to the many persons who provided feedback on portions of the manuscript at various stages of development. The book is better because of them, though responsibility for its shortcomings remains my own. Thank you to Garlinda Burton, Greg Carey, Michelle Daniels, Brian Ellison, Jonette Gay, Julia O'Brien, Suzanne Trapnell, Barbara Day Miller, and participants in classes at Grandview UMC and at Otterbein UMC who beta-tested the manuscript as a group study. Not least, I am grateful to my wife, Myka Kennedy Stephens, who offered vital feedback, encouragement, and support during each stage of this project.

Finally, I would like to thank my former teachers, most especially John Holbert and Roy Heller, who taught me to exegete the Hebrew Scriptures, to see myself in the narrative, to interpret the Word of God in creative and faithful ways, and to preach the Good News.

—Darryl W. Stephens, Eastertide 2017

Contributors

Michael I. Alleman retired from ordained ministry in June of 2015. He is married to Megan Alleman and together they have two sons, Matthew and Christopher. Raised in Elizabethtown, Pennsylvania, Michael grew up on a small farm. He graduated from United Theological Seminary in 1977 with an MDiv. He served Covenant UMC in Lebanon County as associate pastor for seven years, New Holland UMC as lead pastor for ten years, and Grandview UMC as lead pastor for twenty-one years.

Andrea Brown has served at Grandview UMC since 1999. She was this church's associate pastor for fifteen years before becoming co-lead pastor in 2014 and lead pastor in 2015. Before that, she worked as a print journalist. She and her husband, Tim Buckwalter, live in the city of Lancaster, where they raised their two children. She holds degrees from Bucknell University, Columbia University, and Lancaster Theological Seminary.

Ruth A. Daugherty, a freelance educator and consultant, has served on numerous boards and agencies at all levels of the church, including a term as president of the Women's Division (now, United Methodist Women) in the UMC. She has taught in schools of mission and written articles and study guides for various church publications. She is author of *The Missionary Spirit: The History of the Methodist Protestant Church, 1830–1939.*

Mary Merriman is married to Ruth Stetter and lives in Lancaster County. She is ordained clergy (retired) in Metropolitan Community Church and serves Grandview UMC as a visitation pastor.

Darryl W. Stephens is an ordained deacon in the UMC and a transplant to Lancaster County. A life-long Methodist, he grew up in Atlanta, Georgia, and holds a PhD from Emory University. He is currently Director of United Methodist Studies at Lancaster Theological Seminary and author of *Methodist Morals: Social Principles in the Public Church's Witness*. He and his wife, Myka Kennedy Stephens, a consecrated deaconess, have two children.

Abbreviations

LGBTQIA+	lesbian, gay, bisexual, transgender, questioning, queer, intersexual, androgynous, and asexual persons
MCC	Metropolitan Community Church(es)
RMN	Reconciling Ministries Network
UMC	(The) United Methodist Church
UMW	United Methodist Women

Introduction

This is the story of a people on a journey of faith. It is about ancient Israelites learning to trust a God they had forgotten and Moses, the prophet, to lead them out of slavery to a better place. It is about modern-day Christians learning what it means to be the Body of Christ in ministry with all persons, including those of every sexual orientation and gender identity. There are commonalities. There are differences. Presented in parallel, these two stories, past and present, express the unique experiences of a people learning to be God's people. These are the faith-filled testimonies of people both ancient and modern-day.

The story of the Exodus is an ancient one, a defining narrative of biblical faith. We tell this story over and over so that we, like the Israelites, may discover whose we really are. "When in the future your child asks you, 'What does this mean?' you shall answer . . ." (Exodus 13:14a).

We do have an answer, don't we?

We need to share our testimonies. As people of faith, we, as well as our children, need continual reminder of who and whose we are. A ministry filled with compassion and justice for immigrants, widows, orphans, and the poor (Exodus 22:21–25) rests on understanding of our part in God's story. This is the journey of open and affirming ministry with all of God's creation. We are *God's* people.

We tell this ancient story so that we, like the Israelites, may learn over and over how to be faithful to God. Through telling and retelling our story, forgetfulness yields to remembrance and misidentification yields to recognition. Disobedience yields to obedience and groaning yields to faith. We tell this story to remind ourselves who God is, "I am the Lord your God, who brought you out of the land of Egypt, out of the house of slavery" (Exodus 20:2), and what this claim demands of us, "You shall not wrong or oppress a resident alien, for you were aliens in the land of Egypt" (Exodus

1

22:21). This is the story of the people Israel becoming God's people, with profound truths and implications for our lives today. *We* are God's people.

Each generation must discover this identity for itself.

When we find ourselves in the narrative, when we learn to see the world through the eyes of the characters in Scripture, we can learn much about God and ourselves. The Bible is a collection of life-changing stories about God and God's relationship to humanity. The meaning of the text is found in this imaginative interplay between the biblical narrative and the story of our lives. There is grumbling. There is discord. And there is faith in God, whom we know because God has first known us and heard our cries. This is a story for us, as inheritors of this promise. This is about us. We *are* God's people.

Alongside the biblical narrative, the people of Grandview UMC offer their own stories of learning to be God's people in ministry to all persons. The story of Grandview is a recent one. We tell the story of this congregation's journey so that we, like the Israelites, may rediscover, remember, and remind ourselves whose we really are. We are a people learning to be the people of God. We tell the story so that other congregations can rediscover and remember God, who delivers us from slavery to sin, death, and even our own prejudices and hatreds. Ours is a story of listening for God in the wilderness of today.

Our journey has led us to an open and affirming ministry fully inclusive of LGBTQIA+ persons.

> Jesus Christ calls Grandview United Methodist Church to be a fully inclusive church, recognizing the sacred worth of all people, including those of every sexual orientation and gender identity. We embrace those who are marginalized for any reason. Grandview cultivates respectful discussion of differences among all who seek to love their neighbors.[1]

Ours is a story pointing to God, who has accompanied us on this journey. Ours is a story of catching a glimpse of I AM WHO I AM even as we await entry into the promised land, the kin-dom of God, in which we finally and fully recognize our relatedness to all of creation.

We tell this story because we were once strangers in the land of Egypt. Reading our lives through the story of Exodus, we learn that open and affirming ministry transcends LGBTQIA+ inclusion. It is also about race

---

1. Grandview UMC, http://grandviewumc.org. The Reconciling Ministries Network (RMN) offers additional examples: "Sample Reconciling Statements."

relations, poverty, generational change, divorce, immigration, and any other human-created barrier to loving God and neighbor. We are all refugees on the journey of faith, and we find strength in God, who delivers us from captivity. Telling Grandview's story alongside the story of Exodus is our way of claiming the text for ourselves and, we hope, encouraging you to do the same.

The experience of one congregation is hardly comparable in importance to the defining narrative of the Hebrew Scriptures. But Grandview's story is meaningful to us and, we hope, may become meaningful to you— not as a way of drawing attention to this particular congregation but as a way of pointing to God, who accompanies us on the journey. Until we see ourselves in the biblical narrative, until we try on these characters and picture what it must have been like in that time and place, until we risk taking the journey ourselves, the paradigmatic story of Exodus is but a distant echo of a past faith. Animated by our imaginations, though, this story is our story. Our experience of becoming the people of God finds resonance and encouragement in the story of Hebrew slaves and their deliverance. This can be your story, too.

ABOUT EXODUS

The history of interpretation of the Exodus story spans the entire theological spectrum. It is the quintessential story of deliverance from slavery, one that African American slaves in the antebellum U.S. embraced as their hope and that African American congregations still claim as their own. Immigrants through the centuries have found solace and strength in this portion of Scripture. Many oppressed peoples have found grace in this story of God's deliverance—and many conquerors justification for their actions. For example, Afrikaner Nationalism, the movement that created the system of Apartheid in South Africa, appealed to the Exodus story as it drove out native peoples from their homeland.[2] "Exodus" is also the name of an international, "ex-gay" organization that closed with an apology in 2013, after thirty-seven years of attempting to "convert" homosexuals to heterosexuals.[3] Clearly, Exodus has many different meanings to many different people. In this book, we focus on the story and characters in Exodus to understand

2. De Gruchy, *The Church Struggle in South Africa*, 20, 31, 200.

3. Bailey, "Ex-gay Group." However, other international groups still operate out of this framework, for example: http://www.exodusglobalalliance.org.

this narrative in relation to our identity as a Christian community and our own experiences of faith.

Our identity is bound in relationships, with each other and with God. It is not enough that God loves us. It is not enough that God dwells among us. God desires that we also be aware of this reality. As God tells Moses on Mount Sinai, "I will dwell among the Israelites, and I will be their God. And *they shall know that I am the Lord their God, who brought them out of the land of Egypt that I might dwell among them*; I am the Lord their God" (Exodus 29:45–46, emphasis added). It is God's promise and plan that we shall know God and know our origins as God's people. To read the Exodus story as Scripture is to embrace this story as our own.

THE THEOLOGY BEHIND THIS BOOK

You don't have to be Methodist to appreciate and enjoy this book, but it is helpful to know its theological underpinnings. I am a Wesleyan and Grandview is a United Methodist congregation. This theological perspective shapes this book in significant and sometimes subtle ways, though Methodists are not unique in their passion to share how God is acting in their lives.

Methodism is an evangelical movement rooted in traditions of Anglican Catholicism, German pietism, and U.S. imperialism. The United Methodist Church (UMC), the denomination to which I belong, combines these inheritances in complex and conflicted ways, especially as it grapples with how to be in ministry with persons of diverse sexual orientations and gender identities. In this book, I draw upon several foundational Wesleyan principles to present and promote an open and affirming approach to ministry: centrality of Scripture, grace through the activity of the Holy Spirit, faith sharing through personal testimony, and use of the means of grace—particularly Christian conversation in the context of small group accountability.

John Wesley, the father of Methodism, claimed he was "a man of one book." Yet, this Oxford-educated Anglican evangelist studied many texts in addition to the Bible, and he expected his itinerant preachers to study an entire library of spiritual and theological writings that he had abridged for their edification. So, the authority of Scripture remains a central concern for Methodists, even as they debate its relation to other sources of wisdom. In the 1960s, Methodist theologian Albert Outler coined the phrase "the Wesleyan Quadrilateral" to describe the interplay between Scripture, tradition, reason, and experience in Methodist theology. This image has proven a durable, if ambiguous, theological framework for the UMC. What is clear to me, though, is that Scripture is an essential source of wisdom for my faith and that I must bring to my reading of Scripture my entire self—head, heart, and soul. The highest affirmation of the authority of Scripture requires the reader to wrestle with the text in light of Christian tradition (including our history of exclusion, violence, and oppression in the name of God), reason (including our best scientific insights about sexuality and gender), and experience (including the personal testimonies of LGBTQIA+ Christians and the evidence of the Holy Spirit in open and affirming ministries). This book encourages the reader to find God's Word for us today as we read the Exodus story in light of this conviction.

Grace is the quintessential motif of Methodism—and a central tenet of Lutheran and Reformed traditions, as well. Early Methodism spread in England and in North America through preachers who invited their listeners to receive the grace of God through the Holy Spirit. Methodist theologian Randy Maddox describes a Wesleyan understanding of grace as "the uncreated personal Presence of the Holy Spirit."[4] During the Great Awakening of the eighteenth century, evangelists proclaimed grace to everyone, particularly the poor and socially marginalized, through a non-discriminating message of salvation. Men and women learned and taught about God's prevenient grace, which may be thought of as God's election to act in a person's life before that person is ever aware of it. They proclaimed convicting grace, leading a person to confess their sin; justifying grace, setting the soul right with God; and sanctifying grace, allowing a person to grow and mature in their faith. This awakening to the Spirit provoked a rowdy, chaotic time of great social and religious change, not unlike our own.

While the message of salvation is the same, we are learning new ways to proclaim it. This book proclaims a living grace: God is not dead; Christ is risen; and the body of believers is the temple of the Holy Spirit (1 Corinthians 3:16). The Holy Spirit serves as the agent of grace, allowing for new birth and new life in Christ. Whereas earlier evangelists emphasized the need to convict (convince) persons of their sin in order to accept God's pardon, many people today have experienced nothing but condemnation from Christian communities "convicting" them of their unworthiness. For

---

4. Maddox, *Responsible Grace*, 195.

many people today, the most genuine word of grace is to offer a conviction of God's love in a world that so often acts otherwise.

Swept up with unbridled enthusiasm at times, Methodists learned the need to test the Spirit for authenticity. Fellow believers learned to evaluate personal testimony of the Spirit by its fruit. Does this testimony ring true to what I know about God in Jesus Christ? Is it consistent with the good news of forgiveness and reconciliation? Does it contribute to building up the church (1 Corinthians 14:26)? As we experience *charisms*—the gifts of the Spirit (Romans 12:6–8), do we exhibit the marks of a true Christian (Romans 12:9–21)? Once tested, the gifts and experiences of grace in our lives should be celebrated! Methodism was founded by persons experiencing the power of the Holy Spirit in their lives, sharing this testimony with others, and discovering the necessity of mutual support and accountability as they strove to mature in their faith.

Methodists embrace a spectrum of activities conducive to spiritual growth. Wesley promoted participation in the means of grace, ways in which believers may responsibly nurture their own spiritual journey. Based on the Love Commandment, works of piety provide channels for loving God, and works of mercy provide channels for loving our neighbors as ourselves. Thus, searching the Scriptures, prayer, worship, and participation in the sacraments are all means by which we stay in love with God. Likewise, feeding the hungry, visiting those in prison, and all of the other ways that we live out God's compassion and justice are means by which we love our neighbors. Through these channels of grace, we experience the Holy Spirit's presence in our lives. Distinctive among the means of grace, for Wesleyans, is Christian conversation. When Christians gather together in small groups to hold each other accountable in the faith, to support each other's growth in sanctification, and to share testimony, the Holy Spirit is in our midst.

This book is the fruit of such a process—the grace-filled testimony of one congregation experiencing the *charism* of radically inclusive *agape* love through open and affirming ministry. Grandview is still growing into this new reality.

This book is designed to promote awareness of the presence of God: with the ancient Israelites crossing over from slavery to freedom; in the incarnation, Word-made-flesh Jesus of Nazareth; and among individuals and congregations today. When Christians gather into small groups to discuss this book and to share how God is working in their lives, this book may yet be a means of grace. This book is a testimony to the fact that God has created and is still creating. Thanks be to God!

ABOUT THIS BOOK

Out of Exodus emphasizes the theme of being "out." To be in open and affirming ministry is to seek continually to be aware of those who feel left out, singled out, and simply outside the love of God, and then to offer the Good News of Christ. This is a radically evangelistic ministry. It is to proclaim, as does the United Church of Christ, "No matter who you are or where you are on life's journey, you are welcome here." To respond to this Good News is to be called out by God. Together, we set out on a faith journey. To be "out" can mean many things.

This book is shaped around five dramatic acts, each an "out" moment in the drama of our faith story leading to something new. Each act is introduced by Darryl Stephens. Sermons by the Reverends Andrea Brown, Michael Alleman, and Darryl Stephens proclaim these stories in light of Scripture. Responding to each sermon, Ruth Daugherty provides personal reflections from a lifelong ministry as a Methodist layperson. Within each act of this drama, the Reverend Mary Merriman offers personal testimony from her Catholic upbringing and career as a pastor in Metropolitan Community Church (MCC). She shares about experiencing a call to ministry in early childhood, growing up gay, and pastoring two predominantly LGBT[5] churches before arriving at Grandview. Voices of other members of Grandview also contribute testimony throughout the book. Materials in the Appendices offer further guidance and resources for congregations who are on the journey of open and affirming ministry.

Act I, "Crying Out in New Birth," alludes to the cries of the Hebrew slaves at the beginning of the Exodus story. It is a moment of, as Wesleyans say, prevenient grace. God hears and responds to their pain before they are ever aware of God's presence and certainly before they have any recognition of being God's chosen people. The theme of crying out is linked to new birth, both literally and figuratively, in the baby Moses and the formation of Israel as God's people.

Act II, "Called Out to a New Role," alludes to Moses's encounter with God in the burning bush as well as God repeatedly drawing a distinction

---

5. To use the more inclusive expression LGBTQIA+ would be anachronistic in this context.

between Egypt and Israel. Moses is called out to be in leadership; Pharaoh is called out for his treatment of the Hebrew slaves; the people Israel are called out of slavery to worship God in the wilderness. Each character is called out by God to assume a new role in God's story. So are we.

Act III, "Coming Out with a New Identity," links the Passover and crossing of the Sea of Reeds with what it means to come out as "alien" or "queer" in some way. This moment marks a place from which the people Israel cannot turn back, although their self-understanding as God's people is still far from certain. Israel, LGBTQIA+ Christians, and entire faith communities face similar moments of coming out with a new identity.

Act IV, "Figuring Out in a New Voice," offers side-by-side stories of missteps, misrecognition, and misery as Israel and Grandview each find a new voice. From grumblings in the wilderness to the worship of a golden calf to defeat in a church trial, these stories show a people figuring out how to be God's people in a hostile environment. Andrea Brown's "Easter Proclamation," drawn from the Gospel of John and preached in November(!), is an apparent departure from Exodus narrative—and the liturgical calendar. However, as the adopted children of God (Ephesians 1:5) grafted onto the tree that is Israel (Romans 11:17), we find new voice in the saving grace of God in Christ Jesus (always rooted in the Hebrew narrative)—no matter the time of year.

Act V, "Setting Out on a New Journey," prepares us to embark on a new journey of faith and ministry. Michael Alleman, preaching from Deuteronomy, contemplates what it must have been like for Moses to look across to the Promised Land that he will never see. This valedictory on the eve of his retirement from a career in ordained ministry offers hope and encouragement to a congregation that will continue the journey without him as their leader. Andrea Brown, preaching on Good Friday, proclaims a message of responsibility and refuge, drawing on the Gospel of Matthew. For, the way of the cross is the new journey in which we set out as Christians: "we are ambassadors for Christ" (2 Corinthians 5:20).

The book concludes with a short epilogue discussing common challenges to community and ministry, followed by appendices with a glossary and other practical resources for the journey ahead, including discussion questions for group study. For readers interested in the scholarship behind this book, I have written a journal article, published separately.[6]

---

6. Stephens, "A Charismatic Learning."

ACT I

Crying Out in New Birth

"Are you feeling safe yet?"
—Dorothy Garboczi, supportive member, inquiring each week
as Mary Merriman visited Grandview

"I'm grateful to be part of a congregation that seeks to honor all of God's precious children."
—the Rev. Carolene Brubaker, retired clergy and regular attendee at Grandview

"We have no interest in raising our children to accept a faith that puts unreasonable boundaries around God's love. That's why we are grateful to have found Grandview. Its stance as a Reconciling Congregation nurtures the faith we share and want to extend to others."
—Jessica Kahler, member of Grandview

I once experienced a roomful of strangers cry out as the people of God. My wife's friend and seminary classmate, Cameron, had invited us to her wedding. It was our first lesbian wedding, a joyous occasion. Among those present for Cameron and Ann were family, colleagues from work and school, friends from church, and many persons who did not claim any religious connection. We were a diverse group of persons, many of whom had never met before. We were strangers to each other.

It was clear that many of those present had been rejected by a faith community at some point in their lives or had experienced the rejection of family members and friends. During the ceremony, the celebrant, standing before the excited couple and the rest of us, proclaimed a word of grace: "God loves you, and there's nothing you can do about it!" She proclaimed again, a little bit louder: "God loves you, and there's nothing you can do about it!" Caught helpless in the truth of this love, the motley wedding crowd cried out in hope, joy, and pain as the blessing of God washed over us. For a few holy moments, we became the people of God.

Crying out can do this to a people. When we enter that visceral zone of emotion welling up from a lifetime of experience to utter an honest, heartfelt cry—a sigh too deep for words, as Paul says—it becomes a prayer beyond our understanding (Romans 8:26). Yet, God will respond. In fact, God has already responded, even when we are unsure or unaware of God's presence in our lives.

The psalmist knew this truth. The psalms are replete with laments and cries directed to God. "My God, my God, why have you forsaken me? Why are you so far from helping me, from the words of my groaning?" (Psalm 22:1). This psalm gives voice to those of us who feel unloved, left out, and rejected. Yet, the psalmist also declares these raw feelings of hurt on a foundation of deep faith. The psalmist conveys to us the truth that God loves us—and that truth gives us hope. Despite the pain and rejection, despite the uncertainties of each night and day, the Psalmist concludes this prayer with a promise to dedicate her life to God, believing that "future generations will be told about the Lord, and [will] proclaim his deliverance to a people yet unborn" (Psalm 22:30b–31a). We are this people.

The formation of God's people is a matter of origins, new birth. I imagine the covenant with Abraham as the moment of conception of the people Israel. Still nameless as a people, Abram's name will become great through them, and in him "all the families of the earth shall be blessed" (Genesis 12:3). This is the promise of God to form a covenant people, a people not yet born. This is the prior commitment of a loving parent who will hear the cry of a newborn people birthed through slavery in Egypt. This is the love of God for the people of God. "For God so loved the world . . ." (John 3:16)—but I'm getting ahead of the story.

If you've ever witnessed the birth of a child, you know a newborn's cry stirs all sorts of emotions. Joy, relief, hope, expectation, anxiety, and love—unconditional love. As a father, I participated in the birth of my two children, each time holding my wife's hand as she labored to deliver, helping her breathe through each contraction. Our daughter, the younger of the two, emerged with an immediate objection to her brutal entry into the world. Clearly upset with this means of arrival, she wailed through tears unmistakable in their defiance. Something of her personality showed through, even as a newborn. She is still quick to express her dissatisfaction with the injustices of the world. Yet, in the hospital that morning, I could feel nothing but love for this tiny child screaming her way into our hearts. Birthing is a violent, painful process. Most of us were born crying out.

Perhaps my experience as a parent offers some insight into God's response to the cries of the Hebrew slaves at the beginning of the Exodus story. "The Israelites groaned under their slavery, and cried out" (Exodus 2:23b). I imagine this groan as the cry of a people being born. A newborn's cry is not directed to anyone in particular. Yet, "God heard their groaning, and God remembered his covenant with Abraham, Isaac, and Jacob" (Exodus 2:24). As a Wesleyan, I interpret this as a moment of prevenient grace. God hears and responds to their pain before they are ever aware of God's presence and certainly before they have any recognition of being God's chosen people. God, our loving parent, "looked upon the Israelites . . . and took notice of them" (Exodus 2:25). God remembers the covenant, but this newborn people must grow into that awareness and live into what it means.

In Act I, Michael Alleman sets the stage in chapter 1, "Remembering Our Past." He writes about Joseph, the Holocaust as remembered by Elie Wiesel, and a story from his own ministry. In her personal reflections on the same theme, Ruth Daugherty shares how her past has shaped her commitment to justice in church and society. The early witness of Methodist women for racial justice attuned her to work toward "an accepting community for all of God's created humanity." Mary Merriman then recounts her personal testimony, as shared with the Searchers Class at Grandview.

Chapter 2, "Birthing New Life," begins with Andrea Brown's sermon, "The Midwives," in which she tells the story of Shiphrah and Puah, who feared God more than Pharaoh. Theirs is a story that most of us have never heard from the pulpit. The sermon's message is timely for people facing oppression: "One simple act of refusing to cooperate can change everything." In reflection, Ruth Daugherty writes about the pressure to be "born again" at revivals led by her father, a United Brethren preacher. She eventually experienced a new birth in faith—not through the literal reading of Scripture she was taught as a child but through a community of women who freed her to question and discern the relevance of Scripture for today.

Chapter 3, "Nurturing the Vision," shows that it takes a community. Andrea Brown's sermon, "Baby in an Ark," is about the baby Moses but also about us. "It's a story of fear and courage meeting and of courage repeatedly overcoming fear—courage on both sides of the river." Then, Ruth Daugherty shares her own story of nurturing the vision of God's inclusive love as she formed an adult Bible study class at Grandview. Act I concludes with testimony by Mary Merriman, who tells of her role on the front lines of the AIDS crisis in the 1980s, caring for HIV+ newborns and other children.

1

Remembering Our Past
Exodus 1:1–9

"SETTING THE STAGE"
BY MICHAEL I. ALLEMAN

The biblical narrative offers us a foundational view of God and God's people. I'm going to read the Exodus as a story in which the people of Israel are freed from human tyranny to become slaves to their own, loving God. "You shall be my people, and I shall be your God."

The story begins with remembering. Several generations had passed between the death of Jacob, also known as Israel, and the death of Joseph. The beginning of Exodus tells us that when Jacob died, he had *seventy* descendants—a lot from one man. Those descendants had long since died. Generations later, the descendants of Israel, the Israelites who lived in Egypt, numbered over 600,000 males or over a million people. Their number had grown greatly.

"Now a new king arose over Egypt, who did not know Joseph" (Exodus 1:8). Whenever I hear this in the Exodus story, I immediately think of the late Elie Wiesel. Wiesel was a survivor of the Nazi concentration camps and author of over forty books. He spent his entire career retelling the story of those concentration camps. When asked why he would spend his life talking about something so difficult, so painful, he responded by saying,

"If we do not remember our past, we're condemned to repeat it."[1] The text seems to insinuate that if the king had remembered Joseph, he would have acted differently and, in fact, could have changed the whole course of history. If only the Egyptian leader had remembered Joseph's story! Do you remember Joseph? Do *you* remember who Joseph was?

This new king paints a picture where the Israelites have become so numerous and strong that they'll take over. "Look, the Israelite people are more numerous and more powerful than we. Come, let us deal shrewdly with them, or they will increase and, in the event of war, join our enemies and fight against us and escape from the land" (Exodus 1:9–10), implying, "we'll lose our cheap labor." It's a picture of fear. Throughout our Scriptures, we'll hear this reoccurring theme: fear paralyzes while hope liberates and empowers. We'll hear this theme over and over again in the Exodus story.

In my own personal life, whenever I find myself becoming filled with fear, I strive to name the fear. Just naming my fear can somehow take away some of its power. Then, I try to reframe it into something that I hope to happen. Finally, I ask myself, "Where does my hope lie?"

I so clearly remember a time when I was a part of the Pennsylvania Council of Churches that met up in Harrisburg. At that time, the Council was fiercely against state funding of private schools. And in the midst of our discussion, one person brought such clarity to this issue—at least, to my thinking—when she said, "I'm really not nearly so interested in being against something as I'm interested in being *for* something." And she went on to say, "I don't have a passion for being against state funding for private schools, what I do have a passion for is that every child in Pennsylvania gets a quality education regardless of where they live, the color of their skin, or the income of their parents. That's what I'm passionate about." It's not about what I'm against; it's about what I'm for. Hope liberates; fear paralyzes.

If this new king had remembered Joseph, if he had known who Joseph was and what Joseph had done, he would have remembered the wisdom of Joseph to build the storage barns when they had seven years of abundant crops and how it had prepared them, not only to keep the Israelites from starving, but to keep the Egyptians from starving as well during the seven years of drought that followed. And if he had remembered who Joseph was, perhaps he would not have been driven so much by fear as by the

---

1. The quote, "Those who cannot remember the past are condemned to repeat it," is originally attributed to George Santayana.

possibilities, the hope of them possibly working together, a new partnership being formed with the Israelites.

So often in my life, whatever I am in the midst of doing, I find it difficult to see exactly how God is at work in my life. But looking back, looking back over different events, I usually come to see how God was at work in all that was taking place—things I hadn't even noticed before. I don't know about you, but I can't afford to forget my own past, let alone the past of all of those who have gone before me. Because it's only in looking back and remembering that I am filled with renewed hope for what is yet to come.

REFLECTIONS BY RUTH A. DAUGHERTY

"Go forward while looking in the rearview mirror" was advice given when I was learning to drive a car. My husband-to-be was my instructor and constantly questioned me about what was going on behind or around the car, prompting me to keep an eye on the rearview mirror. He emphasized that this was not to see where I had been but to assist me in going forward by viewing what the persons or vehicles were doing that might impact my own actions. This is a good metaphor for my experience as a layperson in ministry through United Methodist Women (UMW) and provides context for our story at Grandview UMC.

United Methodist Women is remembering our past while moving into the future, as we celebrate 150 years as an organization.[2] Focusing on corporate and individual actions, UMW seeks to fulfill our Christian responsibilities to eliminate segregation, abolish child labor, eliminate sex slavery, reduce illiteracy, reform prisons, and work for full human rights and dignity for all persons. All proposals, discussions, and decisions for action initially involve study, reflection, discussion, and prayerful discernment of Scripture, both by staff and the diverse members of our national office (formerly, the Women's Division of the General Board of Global Ministries). Consideration is always given to Scripture and the message it might have for the present time in being faithful to the commandment to love God and love our neighbor. These commitments to social justice have often put us on the frontlines of social change and conflict.[3] I'll share one story as I remember it.

2. United Methodist Women, "150th Anniversary."
3. For some of this history, see Knotts, *Fellowship of Love.*

In 1942, our UMW denominational office, then called the Woman's Division of Christian Service of the Board of Missions and Church Extension of The Methodist Church, planned a national Assembly to meet in St. Louis. Prior to the event, it was discovered that the white members of the Woman's Division were to be housed in a downtown hotel and the African American women were to be housed in the homes of African Americans throughout the city of St. Louis. When inclusive housing arrangements could not be arranged with the St. Louis hotel, the Women's Division forfeited their deposit and moved to Columbus, Ohio, where one hotel could accommodate the racially integrated group. Following that event, the Woman's Division adopted a policy that all members were to be accommodated equally for any future meetings and encouraged the Methodist General Conference to do the same. However, the 1944 General Conference refused to adopt an equal accommodation policy.[4]

These experiences caused me to reflect upon Scripture. The Genesis account of the creation of humanity said nothing about the division of persons into races. Differences mentioned in other scriptural references were based on nationalities or designations of Jews and Gentiles. John 3:16 speaks of God's love for *the world*—a term inclusive of all people.

I resonated with the decisions and actions of Women's Division, and determined to live and act accordingly. While attending Lebanon Valley College in my junior and senior years, I was a member of a racially inclusive Christian group that took programs to churches where we were often given a meal. I shared these experiences with my friends when I was home during college breaks. Some of them were appalled that I would eat at the same table with persons who were not "white."

Sharp criticisms followed many of the actions of the Woman's Division, but predecessor organizations of United Methodist Women continued to work for ordination of women, immigration reform, and civil and human rights for all persons. A Charter of Racial Policies to govern "its own organization and program" was adopted in January 1952,[5] fully eighteen months before the historic 1954 Supreme Court Decision, *Brown v. The Board of Education,* that ended segregation in the public schools. Spurred

---

4. Murray, *Methodists*, 56.

5. Knotts, *Fellowship of Love*, 197. For full text of "Charter for Racial Policies—1952," see Murray, *Methodists*, 267–68.

by the Women's Division, the Methodist General Conference adopted the Charter of Racial Policies in 1964.[6]

However, not all local Methodist churches followed the policies. During a Sunday School class in a Methodist Church in West Virginia, the conversation was about the audacity of the blacks shopping on Saturday night and not getting off the sidewalks where the whites were walking. The lesson was taken from Genesis 9:18–28 about Canaan's curse after seeing the nakedness of Noah. The interpretation given was Canaan's curse was to make him "black" and he and his offspring were to be slaves. This led me to a commitment to find some way to counter this biblical interpretation and to work for an accepting community for all of God's created humanity.

Looking in the rearview mirror of experiences working for justice in church and society, I see value in the processes used by UMW. For me, this has meant beginning with prayer and a biblical and theological basis; securing respected leadership; enlisting others who are committed to bring about change, including persons for whom justice is being sought; developing a process of education, including conversations and discussions with individuals and groups; and embracing the challenge of a possible long-term commitment to accomplish the sought result.

TESTIMONY BY MARY MERRIMAN

I began attending Grandview at a time when they were considering what it means to be open and affirming. I joined the Reconciling Ministries Team, a group of ten or so people who wanted the congregation to become a Reconciling Congregation, and agreed to share my personal story as a lesbian and as a retired clergy member of Metropolitan Community Church. This testimony begins the faith journey I shared.

Church and faith have always been important to me. I grew up Roman Catholic and first realized God's call to ministry in my life when I was about five or six years old. My uncle, who was a Catholic priest and missionary, said Mass for various orders of nuns. He took me along on his visit to a Catholic Order called the Little Sisters of the Poor. I think of it as my first interview for the convent, as it was suggested that I select an order that I might be interested in joining when I got older. After all, that's what every Irish Catholic eldest daughter is to do! I was the eldest daughter of six siblings at the time. We lived in a crowded apartment and actually took up

6. Murray, *Methodists*, 250.

two rooms of the upstairs neighbors' apartment. Staying overnight with the Little Sisters of the Poor in Chicago was quite a treat!

The nuns were gracious hosts. I had a warm bed with two pillows and milk and cookies before I went to sleep. In the morning, one of the nuns came into my room and presented me with a red transistor radio. She said that it was the one personal belonging that she had not yet given up when she became a member of the order. She thought I might like to have it. I treasured it for years. However, the most important gift of that memorable journey was spending time with my uncle, whom I adored. We attended Mass at 6am. I watched my uncle elevate the host during the consecration of communion. Perhaps it was all of the good feelings combined with the mystic holiness that implanted the thought that someday I would like to celebrate communion. Today, communion remains one of the holiest moments in my faith life—as it does for many LGBTQIA+ Christians in Metropolitan Community Churches and other denominations. It is the communal meal that signifies God's love and acceptance through the Incarnate One.

While I didn't become a nun, I did become a minister in the Universal Fellowship of Metropolitan Community Churches (UFMCC, or MCC for short). MCC was founded in 1967 by the Rev. Troy D. Perry after having his credentials removed by his religious denomination when he disclosed his homosexual feelings. Historical accounts of the founding of MCC describe Troy's search for meaning, purpose, and belonging in the context of his faith and abandonment by his church and family. After a period of struggle and a suicide attempt, Troy recounts God's voice saying, "Troy you are my child and I love you." The first meeting of MCC was in his home in Huntingdon Beach, California. It was a worship service attended by twelve people—all gay men. There are now nearly three hundred MCC congregations in twenty-two countries worldwide.[7]

I first attended MCC Baltimore in 1975. My partner at the time and I were seeking to solemnize our relationship and were told that MCC celebrated Holy Unions. The co-pastors of MCC Baltimore were ex-Catholics who had a flair for icons and vestments, which they brought in to the worship experience. Given my Catholic upbringing, the surroundings were comfortable, familiar, and affirming. For a time, I wondered if MCC Baltimore was actually created by the Catholic Church to absolve its sins of preaching a loving God who hated gay people. Of course, that wasn't true.

7. Metropolitan Community Churches, "History of MCC."

MCC is its own authentically called church of Jesus Christ proclaiming God's love for all people.

While the relationship that initially led me to MCC Baltimore didn't last, my love affair with God and the MCC has lasted over forty years. I had found my spiritual home. I began studying to become an MCC clergyperson and was licensed in 1983 and ordained in 1987. During my MCC career as a clergy member, I pastored two MCC congregations—one in Lakeland, Florida, and one in Lancaster, Pennsylvania. Both were difficult ministries given the level of isolation experienced by LGBTQIA+ people, the level of conflict within society, and the limited resources and institutional support for building a church and community within MCC and the gay community at the time.

As a subculture, several bonds of trust characterized our LGBT community (though we were not fully attentive to the needs of transgender persons). These bonds included supporting and caring for one another, keeping each other's secret (not disclosing one's sexual orientation), and growing our faith with one another. Through the 1990s, it was not uncommon for LGBTQIA+ people to have limited support with their families and work community—not disclosing their sexual orientation or gender identity to their families or workplace for fear of rejection. While it's not a very strong framework upon which to build a church, it was often the weakness that magnified the strength of God's love and steadfastness within MCC. Many members would disclose a deep faith and reliance on God to sustain them in difficult times. This became the pillar upon which the church would stand and flourish! Challenges were great, however. Especially challenging were homophobia, HIV/AIDS, and civil and religious rights.

Both of my congregations were small in the beginning. I began my ministry in Lakeland by establishing a new congregation. I was a student clergy person in Tampa MCC and had several contacts with people in Polk County, the next county east of Tampa. In 1982, I decided to explore the possibility of beginning an MCC study group in Lakeland, although unemployment rate was about 20 percent at the time and many of my contacts had moved away. There was one bar in Lakeland called the Green Parrott, at which I routinely met people to talk about faith and loneliness, rejection and acceptance. Out of these contacts, Good News MCC emerged, becoming officially recognized as an MCC congregation in 1983.

2

———

Birthing New Life
Exodus 1:8–22

"THE MIDWIVES" BY ANDREA BROWN

Although the particulars differ in every time and place, Exodus is a very familiar story. Throughout human history, some groups of people have exploited others—treated them as if they are not really even human—even though we're all equal in God's eyes. There are countless examples, right up to human trafficking today—and that's only the most obvious present-day example. Exodus is one of those stories. It is a story about oppression, fear—recognizing it in ourselves and identifying what it is we're afraid of—and even faith. I'm going to tell you the story of two of the most fearless, rogue, hard-core, risk-taking, daredevil, lion-taming, snake-charming, dragon-slaying, strong, determined, feisty, self-confident, unyielding, catalytic people in the entire Bible. I cannot even believe that we don't have a single hymn in our hymnal about them. Shiphrah and Puah are their names.

Their story is told only once in the three-year lectionary cycle used by Protestants. It's omitted entirely from the Roman Catholic lectionary,[1] and it's missing from many versions of the Haggadah, the retelling of the Exodus story at Passover Seders. That's remarkable, because the fact is, the

1. Fox, "Strange Omission of Key Women in the Lectionary," 13.

whole Exodus event—the liberation and everything else that happens in this entire book—would not have happened without what they did first!

We pick up the story with Pharaoh's dawning realization that not everyone around here looks like him anymore. And instead of being happy about it, he freaks out. This happens at other times in history. Groups of people live together in harmony for many centuries and then, for some reason, someone in power decides to divide them: Serbs and Bosnians, Hutus and Tutsis, Syrian Muslims and Syrian Christians. Fear and distrust stack up like the blocks of a pyramid, until the pyramid turns into a volcano, and it erupts. Pharaoh—unnamed because he represents all bad guys (male and female) of all times and places—says to everyone: "We have an Israelite problem." They always say it that way. Hitler said it: "We have a Jewish problem." George Wallace said it: "We have a Negro problem." Some Americans are now saying it: "The problem is all these Spanish-speaking people."

Wrong! The truth is: Germany had a *Nazi* problem. The U.S. had (and still has) a *racism* problem. The problem wasn't the Jews; it was other Germans' attitudes about the Jews. The problem wasn't the black people and it isn't the Mexicans and it certainly isn't Central American children. The problem, quite frankly, is the attitudes and action or inaction of many of the rest of us, stirred up by some loud, leading voices for reasons of their own. Unfortunately, when kings and plutocrats and presidents and warlords and popes and people on TV and radio freak out, things tend to go really, really badly. They do not work out well for the majority of people. So Pharaoh's minions forced the Hebrews into hard labor, slavery. I guess he figured he'd weaken them so much they wouldn't have the strength to rebel.

Now, you may wonder, since the Hebrew people were more numerous and powerful, as Pharaoh said, why didn't *they* attack and destroy the Egyptians? This reminds me of a bit of dialogue between a Jesuit priest and a six-year-old Native American boy in Sherman Alexie's novel *Indian Killer*. Looking at a stained-glass window that depicts the murder of Jesuit missionaries by Indians, the boy asks, "Why didn't the Indians kill all the white people?"

"They didn't have the heart for it," the priest says.

"But didn't the white people kill most of the Indians?"

"Yes," the priest says simply, "they did."[2]

2. Alexie, *Indian Killer*, 14.

Not only did Pharaoh force the Hebrews into hard labor, he also stockpiled weapons and had *them* build the places to hold them. He put his whole heart into it. He was operating out of a deep-seated fear of the other, though at this point, the other wasn't harming anybody. The only ones doing harm were Pharaoh's people—the Egyptians. Maybe what they really feared was something deep inside themselves.

Is that what is going on when we put so many black people (and males in particular) in prison? Do we fear their becoming more numerous and powerful? Is this why we can't pass sensible immigration reform—even though it's supported by businesses as well as religious and humanitarian groups? The fear of the other drives us into some very dark places in our own souls; it can cause us to take some pretty terrible and terrifying actions. However, in the Exodus story, Pharaoh's tactic had an ironic result: "the more they were oppressed, the more they multiplied and spread . . ." (Exodus 1:12). The Egyptians became more and more ruthless, and the Hebrews just became stronger.

Now, it's important to remember that Pharaoh *alone* did not enforce the rules. The rules could not have been enforced without the cooperation of a whole bunch of people—a whole bunch of people who obeyed him and carried out his orders, no matter how horrible they were. It's quite possible that these "taskmasters" even included some Hebrews, since members of oppressed groups often get co-opted like that in such perverse situations. And then, of course, the other people who made it possible were a whole bunch of Egyptians who just looked the other way. Pharaoh really couldn't have carried out his malicious plans without them.

I wonder how those Egyptians (and maybe a few Hebrews) felt about treating their neighbors so cruelly—beating them if they took a break from working, giving them very little food and water as they worked out in the sweltering sun all day, essentially stealing their labor by reaping the benefits of it without paying them much. Maybe some liked having so much power. Probably some felt much more uncomfortable. But by the fourteenth verse of Exodus, that part of the story is over. The main story of the Exodus starts in 1:15. It starts the moment when a handful of people begin to *disobey*—to stand up. And it starts with two midwives, Shiphrah and Puah.

These women's defiance sets off the whole chain of events. Before there were drowning armies or parting waters or locusts or hail or frogs—before there was even Moses—there were Shiphrah and Puah. And without Shiphrah and Puah's defiance, there would not have *been* a Moses—nor frogs, nor hail, nor locusts, nor parting waters, nor drowning armies, nor freedom. So, who were they?

Well, there are two possible interpretations: Shiphrah and Puah are either "Hebrew midwives" or Egyptians who serve as "midwives to the Hebrews." Some readers assume they're Egyptian, because why would Pharaoh ever think he would get a couple of Hebrews to kill their fellow Hebrews? If that's the case, this is an awesome story of two "insiders" refusing to cooperate with their own leaders in order to save the "outsiders." Privileged people reaching out to the oppressed. It's an Oskar Schindler story. A Thaddeus Stevens story. (Stevens was an abolitionist congressman from Lancaster.) Such stories are awe-inspiring. But the more likely possibility is that Shiphrah and Puah (whose names are Semitic, not Egyptian) are Hebrews and that Pharaoh is just that dumb or that arrogant—just that drunk on his own power and just that used to being able to get his way— that he thinks he can even order Hebrews to kill their fellow Hebrews. And that's what he tries to do.

He calls the midwives in and says: "When you go to help a Hebrew woman give birth, if it's a boy, kill him. If it's a girl, let her live." (Later on, when *this* plan fails, he calls on everyone to drown all the baby boys in the Nile.) I doubt he wanted to let the girls live for compassionate reasons; I'm sure his reasons were nefarious. But at any rate, it was a huge tactical error to view girls and women as non-threats. If they had tossed the *girls* in the river, Miriam wouldn't have been there to save her little brother Moses and work out a deal with the Princess. But we're getting ahead of ourselves.

Let's be clear: what was going on here was genocide. It can be hard to see evil when you're standing right up next to it. Beating people while working them with no concern for their wellbeing and little compensation—that came from a genocidal impulse, too. But it had more subtlety to it. There's nothing subtle about killing babies. That's unambiguously evil, and the God-fearing midwives were not about to do it. Their allegiance to God and to godly principles of right and wrong was higher than their allegiance to any person, even the king.

Simply put, they stopped fearing Pharaoh. They "feared" God instead—not the way one fears an abusive parent (that was how people feared Pharaoh) but the way one fears to disappoint a loving parent. They didn't want to disappoint God by living in a way that didn't square with God's way. Powerful and deadly as Pharaoh was, they realized there's a Higher Power, and they chose to be *its* subjects instead. That was the pivotal moment—not just for them but also for the whole community. It was a Rosa Parks moment, a Ruby Bridges event. It was a catalyst for all that came afterward.

Can you imagine! Can you imagine being hauled in front of the king after directly disobeying his order?! What would you do?

What these midwives did was ingenious. They turned Pharaoh's own ignorance, his own flawed thinking, against him. It's "a common racist notion [that] . . . the Other is closer to Nature" or has some sort of "animal-like" superpower: that they are more *different* than *like* us.[3] So the midwives said, "Those Hebrew women, they're not like Egyptian women. They're vigorous." (The Hebrew word means, "beastly, like the animals in the field.") "They're so strong they give birth before we can even get to their houses." Pharaoh bought it: hook, line, and sinker.

This is the kind of story we love to tell: sticking it to the Pharaohs of the world. Can you believe this guy? He's not so all-wise and all-powerful after all! I'm sure this story is one that got requested around the campfire a lot. Terence Fretheim does a great job of pointing out how funny it is, how pregnant with delicious ironies: "two Hebrew midwives outwit the king of all Egypt"! The king "stoops to converse" with little ol' Shiphrah and Puah because he can't "move his intentions forward" without *their* help. " . . . Pharaoh can get the entire Egyptian community to bend to his will but fails to get two daughters of Israel to so respond." *They're* remembered by name; *he's* the nameless one.[4] Presaging Herod, Pharaoh doesn't even pick on people his own size; he feels threatened by babies! And he, big and mighty, is then bested by two "little people." Fretheim continues, "These women are not leaders of the community, persons in a position of influence who could have an impact on governmental policy."[5] Often, ironically, the most powerful actions come from those who start out with the least power. It is amazing whom God chooses to empower. It is amazing whom God manages to empower.

Early Jewish folklore magnified the irony further. The rabbis say that the midwives "not only refused to harm the Hebrew babies, but they actually acted with greater kindness toward them than before."[6] If a baby were born to a poor family, the midwives would go around asking other families for food to sustain it. "In this way the midwives not only saw to it that the

3. Pardes, *Countertraditions in the Bible*, 82.

4. Fretheim, *Exodus*, 31.

5. Ibid., 33.

6. Williams, *The Storyteller's Companion to the Bible*, 27.

children were *born* alive, but they made sure that the youngsters were *kept* alive as well."[7] In so doing, I would note, they also strengthened the community's ties, and that is what allowed the Exodus to succeed. As Louie Crew, a gay Episcopal priest, notes, "Despised tribes survive by being better organized than those who despise them."[8]

The Exodus story is a glorious reminder that the Pharaohs of the world are always doomed to fail. They can be knocked down by the littlest people, using the glue of the Holy Spirit to stick together. One simple act of refusing to cooperate can change everything. A simple act of "creative disobedience."[9] Because of the midwives' actions, Walter Brueggemann observes, "the Hebrew barrio became a future-infested place."[10] If they could do it, people thought, so could we. Come to think of it, if they did it, so can we.

REFLECTIONS BY RUTH A. DAUGHERTY

"You must be born again!" was heard frequently at revival services when I was a child. The sermons were preached by my father, a United Brethren preacher. God was mostly described as a strict judge, punishing and sending people to eternal damnation for their disobedience if they did not confess and follow the Scriptures as they were written. In fact, one of the sermons was "A Trip to Hell and Back" illustrated on a chalkboard carried from rural church to rural church in Virginia. When I read the Bible—a daily requirement—I found an image of God, especially in the prophets and the teachings of Jesus, as loving, forgiving, and accepting. I dared not acknowledge openly that I was questioning the interpretation being preached for fear of retribution.

Attending a mission camp for Otterbein Guild Girls (a youth organization of the Women's Society of World Service of the United Brethren Church), I heard a missionary, Dr. Mabel Silver, speak about her work in Sierra Leone. She spoke of God's love and her love for the people, her ministry of healing, and teaching others so they could become the healers. I saw a person believing in and living the understanding that I had about God and what is expected of us as Christians. I planned to be an educator,

7. Williams, *The Storyteller's Companion to the Bible.*

8. Crew, "Queer Eye for the Lectionary."

9. Fretheim, *Exodus,* 32.

10. Brueggemann, "Variations from the Barrio," 264.

and after hearing Dr. Silver, I determined to respect each student as a child of God and to assist and encourage the potential that each had been given. When I became an English teacher, I had each student write an essay about family, some life experience, and a hope or dream. Then I made a card for each student with the essay information to help me know about each one's experiences, interests, and how to assist them in the learning process.

I still struggled with questions about how to understand some of the passages of Scripture that I had been taught to take literally, such as the whale swallowing Jonah. A professor of Bible at Shenandoah College in Dayton, Virginia, spoke with me about my struggles. He said that Scriptures should have meaning for us, not just as stories or accounts of events. He said the important focus is what is being communicated by the story, not its literalness. That freed me to continue to struggle with the meaning of Scripture without the guilt of accepting every word literally.

Years later, during the eight years that I served as a director of Women's Division, I truly felt I was "born again." I experienced a new life of freedom to question beliefs; to read Scripture, praying for the guidance of the Holy Spirit to discern the relevance for today; to dialogue with persons without being condemned if I differed with their views; to appreciate the diversity of humankind; to work in community for justice for the oppressed and marginalized after intensive study of the issues; and to value the leadership of persons like Theressa Hoover, Associate General Secretary of the Women's Division of the Board of Global Ministries.

Theressa Hoover frequently talked about "Jesus sitting on my shoulder" when speaking about faith and obedience to the commission of Jesus Christ in our times and experiences. As the first African American woman to attain an executive position in the Methodist church, she was an avid advocate for full inclusiveness. This was implemented in the Division with the requirement that all teams of women trainers or groups sent as official delegates or visitors to other countries were to be racially inclusive. This was also a policy for the national officers. Special training for implementation of Racial Justice Policies was given in conferences and local units of United Methodist Women. I have tried to follow these policies when I have had various leadership positions in the church or community.

When I moved to Lancaster in the late 1990s, I looked for a church community with a culture open to questioning for deeper understanding of God; to listen to and discuss diverse views; to be nurtured through study and sermon messages; to be supported in activities of justice; and to be challenged to use time and abilities to bring about needed change for full inclusiveness.

While attending the new members class at Grandview UMC, Pastor Michael Alleman spoke about the culture of inclusiveness at Grandview—where members have diverse views on issues but engage in conversations with respect for one another. He referenced the paragraphs in *The Book of Discipline* of The United Methodist Church under "The Present Challenge to Theology in the Church." These paragraphs speak of "a common desire to participate in the creative and redemptive activity of God."[11]

Grandview provided the place and the space for the continuation of the new life I had experienced. Almost immediately upon joining Grandview UMC, I was asked to lead a Bible study class on Sunday morning, giving me the opportunity and challenge to be with others continuing to search for the meaning and relevance of Scripture for today. This has led to a commitment to full inclusiveness related to race, gender, and sexual orientation both in the church and community.

11. UMC, *The Book of Discipline 2016*, 89.

3

Nurturing the Vision
Exodus 2:1–10

"BABY IN AN ARK" BY ANDREA BROWN

Remembering Joseph. Shiphrah and Puah. The baby in an ark. These initial stories in Exodus are often overlooked, yet they are so foundational to the whole freedom narrative. For instance, it'll be important to know, when we get to the plague stories and we begin to feel sorry for the Egyptians being drenched in blood and darkness and attacked by gnats and locusts, that what led to all that was that the Israelites were enslaved and were the targets of genocide. They were beaten and starved and treated as sub-humans and then Pharaoh forced them to murder half their children— all the boys.

It's also important to know what caused those horrible conditions to begin to change, to find the catalyst that ignited the whole chain of freedom events. These stories remind us that many people have a role to play when change is needed; that whenever our own lives are bad (whether because of sickness or problematic relationships or injustices—whatever), we don't need to sit around waiting for a knight in shining armor to appear. Moses didn't do it alone and there was a reason that so many people were willing to follow his lead, despite the risk.

Part of the reason was the brave, heroic actions of a few specific people who were the first to stop cooperating with Pharaoh. By their actions, they inspired others to stop accepting abuse, to stop tolerating evil, and to stop being a part of it. They prepared the way for Moses. Two midwives, Shiphrah and Puah, sparked the Exodus by bravely defying Pharaoh. The story of the baby in an ark is similar.

Because of the midwives' refusal to murder the Hebrew boys at birth, Moses's mother got a look at him when he was born (Exodus 2:2). She took one look at her newborn, and she said, "He is fine!" That's a lot like what God said when looking at God's brand-new creation: "This is good!" Pharaoh had ordered that all the baby boys should be drowned in the Nile, but Moses's mother—Jochebed was her name—saw Moses and she was no more going to drown her fine creation than God was ever about to let God's good creation be destroyed. Even when humanity almost destroyed itself through meanness and violence, God stepped in to give it a fresh start. God had Noah build an ark, by which humanity was saved from extinction. Well, Jochebed built Moses an ark. The word that's used for Moses's basket is the same word that's used for Noah's ark. It's the only other time that word is used in the whole Bible.

She kept her baby with her as long as she could—three months—but then he was getting too big to hide. So she built an ark, an ark that would save a person, Moses, who, like Noah, would save the people from extinction. (It's interesting, isn't it, that the manger that cradled Jesus looked a bit like an ark or a basket, as well—an unconventional vessel for holding one who comes to save the rest of us.) But then Jochebed had to do the most horrible thing a mother could ever have to do. She had to let her baby go, not knowing whether he would live or die. She coated that basket-ark with bitumen and pitch, like a boat, and she probably hoped that he would float north to freedom.

We can only imagine how terrified Moses's sister, Miriam, must have been as she hid among the reeds, watching to see what would happen to her baby brother. We may have some cutesy Sunday-school images of this scene in our minds, but let's be clear: it's very unlikely that either Miriam or the Princess were smiling in this moment (and it's even more unlikely that the baby was pale and blonde, as often depicted). And the baby wasn't smiling, either. The story tells us he was crying, and that's probably what attracted the Princess and her party to him. (She didn't actually go down into that mucky water to check on him; she sent her maid.)

The Princess immediately knows what's going on: "This must be one of the Hebrews' children," she says (Exodus 2:6). Her words indicate that she knew the situation: her father, Pharaoh, had ordered that these babies should be drowned in the Nile. So, she must have been afraid of what she was about to do, as well as convinced that she *needed* and *wanted* to do it. Thank God that teen-agers do *not* always obey their parents.

Shiphrah and Puah, it seems, were either both Egyptians or both Hebrews—probably Hebrews—but here, it is clear, the two girls on either sides of the Nile are, well, from opposite sides of the river. This time, the saving action requires cooperation and collaboration between insiders and outsiders, between a person in a position of oppression and a person in a position of privilege.

So here is Miriam, the little Hebrew girl, stepping out of the reeds to speak to the Egyptian princess. Didn't her knees tremble, didn't her heart race, as she pushed through the bulrushes to reveal herself and speak: "Shall I go and get you a nurse from the Hebrew women to nurse the child for you?" (Exodus 2:7).

The Princess was no dummy. I can only imagine that she knew exactly what was going on. Surely, she could have found an Egyptian wet nurse for this baby. But she did the bravest and most loving, humanitarian thing: she, knowingly, I believe, sent the baby back to his own mother. She claimed him as her own only to protect him; she was not seeking to steal him. Her motive is like the motive of those loving, adoptive parents who do not take children away from their families or home cultures out of a selfish desire to acquire a cute plaything but out of a tender desire to cooperate with the birth parents in protecting the child and doing what is best for him or her, given bad circumstances.

How much must Jochebed's heart have broken all over again when she had to send the weaned child to the palace! And yet her heart must also have been glad, for she knew this was the only way her son would grow and thrive, and she had learned that the Princess was someone she could trust to protect Moses, even though he would be living right under Pharaoh's nose.

This is a story of desperate times and desperate measures. It's a story of fear and courage meeting and of courage repeatedly overcoming fear—courage on both sides of the river. The story echoes back and echoes forward, making many pairs:

- A Levite man and a Levite woman.

- A daughter of Israel on one side of the river; a daughter of Egypt on the other.

- Bulrushes—a sea of reeds—parting, as Miriam's face peeks out to check on her baby brother; the Red Sea—or was it the Reed Sea?—that would part as the people, led by Moses and Miriam, walked through to freedom.

- The baby Moses crying; the adult Moses crying for freedom.

- A name bestowed: Moses—"drawn out of the water"—just as the one bearing that name would draw his people out through the water.

To understand this Exodus and all Exoduses properly, we need to appreciate these pairings and the value of forging partnerships across our own Nile Rivers. We are called to form conspiracies for good, conspiracies for freedom.

Something like this happens whenever and wherever our youth and adults make homes warmer, safer, and drier. To bring freedom from crushing poverty, people agree to pair up across the Nile River that divides suburban America from rural America. To do it right, for the conspiracy to succeed, the conversation needs to be respectful. So the Appalachia Service Project (ASP) staff teaches volunteers to mosey on Monday—not to come in with sledgehammers a-blazin'—but to take the time to learn what the homeowners value.

The homeowners take a risk to peer out of the bulrushes and let a bunch of mostly unskilled people work on their home and see everything about where they live. On this most recent trip, one of the homeowners opened up the door of her son's room to our crew—a door she had not opened since he died two years ago. To share that place and that tender place in her heart with strangers was a very courageous step.

A few years ago, Dr. Christi Stewart and I reached out across the artificial boundaries that sometimes divide science and religion to care for Daythal Kendall in the last stages of his cancer. It was helpful that Christi is a committed Christian and that I am very fond of science and medicine, so we were each able to speak each other's language. The partnership we formed to try to send Daythal floating safely into eternal life challenged and exhausted us both at times, because dying is not easy for one who is used to fighting to stay alive—one who felt he was not done living his incredibly abundant life here on Earth. But I don't think that either Christi or I, or the

Kendalls, regret that we worked on that together. And in the end, I think, Daythal did feel freed to go.

And I think of the other people around us in that time, too. I think of the adult ASP'ers who came over during Advent—that season of waiting—to share Communion with Daythal. I think of Jonathan Stewart filming the Christmas Eve services for him. Freedom is never achieved through the work of one person or even two. What is needed is not so much a hero as a tender-loving, hope-filled mob.

I'm convinced that it's worth it to push our way through the reeds and to wade into the waters that separate us—to take a risk that someone on the other side may help us to achieve our goals, to keep our eyes open for brave people with like minds who are worthy of our trust. If something or someone is worth saving—if there's a goal worth achieving—then our unseen partner will be God.

Who or what is in your basket? Where is your Nile, and who, by God's grace, is standing on the other side of it, ready to take your hand?

REFLECTIONS BY RUTH A. DAUGHERTY

When I was guest speaker at a church one Sunday morning, the bulletin had me listed as "quest" speaker. It struck me as a fitting adjective for I was, indeed, on a quest to seek the truths in Scripture.

Years later, Pastor Michael Alleman told me several members had requested a Bible Study class to be held Sunday mornings and asked me to form and lead the class. I agreed, with the understanding that the study would begin with an overview of the Bible and be followed by looking at the themes throughout the Scriptures rather than focusing on a few verses at a time. It was my hope that those joining the class would be companions in the quest involving the Scriptures. The class chose "Searchers Class" as its identity, acknowledging we were all seeking to learn more of God's word and will for us today.

Each Searchers class begins with sharing of joys and concerns followed by a prayer of thanks for the joys and supplication for the concerns and closed with all praying:

Open our ears that we may hear,
Open our minds that we may understand
Open our hearts that we may receive your Word for us. Amen

The class agrees upon some basic principles. As leader, I provide supplemental information, utilizing my late husband's commentaries and other sources on the topics being studied; each member receives a copy of the book being used with the Bible study; assigned readings are given for each session for reflection and basis of class discussion; differences of opinions or understandings by any member are respected and not condemned or criticized; and when a statement is made by a member, it is owned by the group and not referenced with the person's name who made it.

The Bible is always the primary source, but resources by theologians and biblical scholars are also utilized. The first resource was *The Bible in Time: A Chronological Exploration of 130 Passages* by Stephen Travis. The author wrote the book to give people a sense of the Bible as a whole and to introduce the themes of biblical faith. Discussion focuses on what is actually said in the Bible and how people have been impacted by God's call on their lives.

As I prepare the background material studying the settings, history, cultures and languages of the passages, I find myself searching more diligently for answers to my questions. For example, what is the core meaning of the two creation stories in Genesis?

As I prepared this lesson, the verse that caught my attention was Genesis 1:26, "Then God said, 'Let us make humankind in our image, according to our likeness . . . .'" Then I remembered a painting by William Zdinak entitled "In His Image" that I had given to my husband for a wedding anniversary gift. It spoke to me of the inclusiveness of humanity, and I wondered if the class members would have a similar experience. I took the painting to the class, placing it at a distance from the members. The painting was the face of Jesus. I carried the painting closer to the class until they could see the face was composed of the faces of famous personalities, family members, Africans, Asians, Indians, men, women, children, and youth. The artist said it didn't matter which persons were depicted because we are all one in Jesus Christ. Viewing and discussing the painting began a process of thinking about what it means that all persons are created with God's spirit and of considering how we interact with the differences that we see.

As the Bible study continued, questions were raised about some of the laws and edicts especially in the Hebrew Scriptures. Slavery was not condemned, but none of us condone that practice today. Other laws about foods, clothing, purification rites, etc. are not considered to be applicable for us today. However, the application of the verses condemning homosexuality brought questions by class members—questions with which I had struggled in years past.

A resource used by the class to address some of these questions was *Making Sense of the Bible: Rediscovering the Power of Scripture Today* by Adam Hamilton. Many in the congregation were wrestling with what the Bible says, especially about homosexuality. Some members of the wider congregation joined in the study of the book. The chapter on homosexuality and the Bible provided a basis for some intensive and intentional discussion. Our quest to discern God's intent for humanity led to a commitment to challenge Grandview to become a welcoming congregation, embracing all of humanity.

TESTIMONY BY MARY MERRIMAN

In 1984, gay men living in Lakeland, Florida, began dying from a mysterious disease. The scientific name of the disease evolved from GRID (gay-related immune deficiency, June 1982) to AIDS (acquired immune deficiency syndrome, September 1983) to HIV (human immunodeficiency virus, 1986).[1] Over time, care for the victims of the disease also evolved from cruelty to compassion.

Symptomatic of cruelty, early on the disease was labeled as the "gay plague." There were no treatments and no desire or will to provide care and comfort when HIV/AIDS first emerged. In my role as an MCC church pastor, I'd go to the Health Department director demanding that he declare a health emergency on behalf of dying gay men. Each time, he would refuse, and we would wait for news of another death. Again, I would return with the same plea. Unless the director would declare a health emergency, funding would not become available for education and advocacy. After eleven deaths, the Polk County Health Department acknowledged our request and began to work with me, MCC, and other community members to reach out to those most affected by this disease. Good News MCC worked with local community members to create Polk County's first and foremost AIDS advocacy organization—Polk AIDS Support Services (PASS). In the ensuing years, Good News and PASS would become known locally as the citadel of information regarding AIDS.

In 1985, the Polk County Children and Youth Agency approached me as a gay community leader to provide assistance in finding homes for

---

1. AVERT, "History of HIV and AIDS Overview."

children with AIDS. The county had not had any children with AIDS born up to that time but they knew the time would come and probably soon. Drug trafficking was a great problem in Polk County, as was homophobia, racism, prostitution, and fear—above all, fear of AIDS. After extensive efforts to persuade existing foster families to care for AIDS children, no foster families were found. In discussions with the Children and Youth Agency, I explained that the people to whom I would be reaching out were lesbian, gay, and bisexual men and women. The agency understood and agreed that they would focus on an applicant's ability to provide the needed care for a child rather than on sexual orientation.

Recruiting foster parents in the gay community was not much easier. Work schedules, uncertainties, and fears stood in the way. Despite those barriers, my partner, Jan, and I opened the first home for children with AIDS in Polk County, taking in Marie, who was born in 1986, and Gail, who was born in 1987. Both girls' moms were sex workers who had drug addictions. Marie's mom eventually died from AIDS, and Gail's mom was in prison. Both babies were born addicted to cocaine and in withdrawal and both tested positive for HIV. Marie lived in a large metal crib for the first two weeks of her life; hospital caregivers typically wore masks, gloves, and gowns when caring for her. When she came to our home, Marie was initially frightened when seeing our smiles or feeling human touch for the first time, as we did not wear masks, gloves, and gowns unless we felt that a situation called for that level of disease control. During her two-week hospitalization, Marie experienced physical withdrawal from cocaine.

Marie was four months old when Gail joined our family. Gail had a much more difficult and protracted time recovering from cocaine addiction after her birth. She developed colic and was inconsolable in her pain. She would drop off to sleep after only sipping an ounce of formula. Consequently, Gail was constantly being fed or sedated with morphine for her pain. One feeding would typically last two to three hours as we cajoled her to consume a minimal amount of food.

At the time, there were no standards for caring for HIV babies, and the only direction we had been given was to keep them free from infection. Their beds, dressers, clothing, toys, and any area with which they had contact were wiped down daily in our home with a 10 percent bleach solution. Consequently, their clothes would shred easily, and even furniture took on a milky kind of haze from the bleach. When a trip to the local hospital was necessary, we were directed to a personal waiting area, either sitting on the floor behind file cabinets away from others in the emergency department or in a broom closet that was emptied except for a chair or two for seating. While the closets seemed a cruel irony, these accommodations were thoughtfully provided by daring and caring staff in the hospital trying to protect the girls from exposure to germs.

Medical care was difficult to access especially due to the bias of the County Health Department director. For instance, we sought care at the Health Department for Marie, who had developed welts on her legs. Jan waited in the treatment room with Marie. The physician came no closer to Marie than the door. From across the room, he observed the welts on a not yet one-year-old baby and started yelling, "Kaposi's! Kaposi's!" (referring to Kaposi's Sarcoma, a type of cancer characterized by purple blotches on the skin). He then demanded that Jan leave the facility and take the baby to the University of South Florida (USF) in Tampa, which was forty miles away. Jan did so, as there were no alternatives. However, the diagnosis was far from cancer. Rather, Marie was diagnosed with spider bites, which she acquired from an old cabinet that sat near her baby swing. To say the least, we never went back to the County Health Department for the babies' care and instead had the children treated at USF. We also got rid of the source of the spider infestation!

Fear was rampant. In Avon Park (located one county south of Polk), a local church leader announced a prayer and community vigil in a local rodeo arena. The purpose of the vigil was to discuss the presence of a family with three young boys diagnosed with AIDS, acquired from a blood transfusion. It was not intended as a call to compassion but rather as an apocalyptic sign of the end times! A short time after the rodeo gathering, the boys' family home was burned to the ground, and the family was forced to leave the community. We, too, became concerned for the safety of our foster children and ourselves. My partner and I arranged for alternate housing should our home be burned. Living in a household with HIV/AIDS in those days meant keeping quiet about our foster babies' condition and our location, resulting in more isolation.

While our MCC family offered a good deal of support, it was very small, and the task of caring for these special-needs children was overwhelming. Nonetheless, courageous, caring, and compassionate members provided babysitting and household support, as needed. Both of our biological families lived 1000 miles away. While I was still getting reacquainted with my family following ten years of estrangement, my dad died in September of 1986, just four months before Marie was born. The same week that we accepted Marie into our home, Jan's parents were en-route to visit us in Lakeland, Florida. We felt that we had to reveal the nature of our foster daughter's illness and did so on the phone. On hearing the news of Marie's coming to our home, they cancelled their visit and returned to Illinois.

ACT II

Called Out to a New Role

"I'm excited to be part of a congregation that is open to people, where people don't have to worry about, 'How do we find a pastor that can understand us?' It's exciting to be part of a congregation that welcomes people of all kinds."

—Rev. Dorothy Killebrew, retired, now attending Grandview

"I wanted to affirm for the folks of Grandview the importance of even reaching this point, as it said a lot about them as a church—a church willing to broach difficult and important issues that many would not even discuss. It showed me how deep their spirituality and theology really went in loving their neighbor with the love of God."

—Kirstin Shrom-Rhoads, Coordinator of Discipleship at Grandview, recalling the congregation's vote to consider themselves open and affirming as a Reconciling Congregation

"As I have gotten to know people who are different from me, I have come to appreciate God's creative diversity. I am also deeply concerned by people's stories of harsh, unkind treatment simply because of who they are. Christ calls us to be especially hospitable to people who are treated unfairly."

—the Rev. Carolene Brubaker, retired clergy and regular attendee at Grandview

Being called out to a new role can be temporary or life-altering. In seminary, I had a friend who worked in the student housing office with me. Christian was (and still is) HIV+. When our boss learned of his status, Christian's job was in jeopardy. Christian told me he was being forced out, and I felt called to act. I wrote a lengthy letter to the dean about the situation, imploring him to act justly (and to avoid an unnecessary lawsuit). My quick action made a difference. The dean intervened; Christian kept his job; and I had assumed a new role, for a day. Answering this call to be an advocate for Christian was not in itself a life-altering event for me. Sometimes a call is just a task. However, when years of everyday calls aggregate into the experiences that shape and refine our moral character, we are changed. We become who God would have us to be, in whatever role we find ourselves.

I have grown into my role as "Reverend" over many years. My call to ministry was not a burning bush experience. Unlike Moses, I did not hear God's voice bellowing to me from a fiery mountainside. The drama of being called out by God consisted (and still consists) of a series of subtle proddings, nudges, and invitations. I grew up in a United Methodist congregation in Georgia that allowed room for questions. There were a lot of folks in this community, mentors for me, living out St. Anselm's motto, "faith seeking understanding." My fourth-grade Sunday School teacher, Mrs. Malone, would call on me to read Scripture aloud in class. Our pastor, Dr. Minter, taught me big words about God during our confirmation class in sixth grade. I learned that God is omnipotent, omnipresent, and omniscient. After my class, I would go to my mother's adult class, the Seekers, since they always ran late, absorbed in discussion. They would let me listen in. Here, I heard adults questioning the Bible, arguing different interpretations of the faith, and pressing each other to dig deeper in their faith. I learned that questions were part of faith; doubts were an invitation to the journey.

Not only did the Seekers class allow me to listen to them, they were also eager to listen to me. When their discussion was over, individual members, many of whom had children my age, would ask about my experience in confirmation class. What was I learning? Did I feel I had a choice in this ritual leading to full church membership? It was as if John Wesley's spirit were there, whispering, "How goes it with your soul?"

I took the membership vows with my sixth-grade class that year, even though I felt I didn't have much choice about it. Not to participate in confirmation would have been a choice not to attend Sunday School for a year, severing me from this faith community. I already knew enough about my faith to know that the congregational community was essential to my growth. I chose to stay, confessing truths I barely understood and with which I still grapple. I did not know it then, but this community of faith was already setting me on the path of theological inquiry, eventually leading to seminary and ordination to the specialized ministry of teaching.

As open as this congregation was to questions and study, sexuality was not part of the discussion. We lived in the Deep South, and there were certain things you just didn't talk about. For example, our choir director was a gay man in a partnered relationship. He was a beloved member of this faith community, bringing joy and artistry to worship every week, and nurtured a generation of musicians in our church. Yet, no one has ever mentioned his sexual orientation in my presence, even to this day. So, I was given the tools of theological inquiry and the experience of inclusive love, but I had to go elsewhere to learn how to put them together in in the context of open and affirming ministry.

Our friend Cameron, whom you met in Act I, also had to go elsewhere. Called out by God for ordained ministry, she attended seminary with my wife, Myka. Both were candidates for ordination in The United Methodist Church. Cameron was serving a church as youth pastor, a ministry she really enjoyed and for which she exhibited many gifts. One Sunday evening, before they were married, Cameron and Ann were dining in a restaurant with Ann's two boys. Some people from Cameron's church saw them there, eating dinner as a family. By the next morning, Cameron's district superintendent had called her in to his office, demanding her resignation as youth pastor and withdrawal from candidacy. She was being called out as a lesbian in a denomination that did not accept her for who she is. God was also calling her out to a new role, as clergy in the United Church of Christ, in which she has thrived.

*   *   *

In Act II, we hear many instances of being called out and many examples of new roles. Andrea Brown opens chapter 4, "Growing Up," with a sermon interweaving the stories of Moses's young adulthood and William Parker's leadership in the Christiana Rebellion, an uprising in violation of the Fugitive Slave Act of 1850. Ruth Daugherty reflects on the love commandment in light of justice, asking, "How am I faithful to God in the way that Jesus taught and lived?" Grandview members Connie Brown and Marge

Cumpston add their voices, discussing sexuality education at church, both intentional and unintentional.

Chapter 5, "Encountering the Sacred," begins with a sermon on the call of Moses, in which Michael Alleman considers the riskiness of standing on holy ground. Ruth Daugherty offers her own reflection on encountering the sacred in a church parking lot—an event that changed not only her views on homosexuality but also the way she listens to persons whose views differ from her own. Grandview members Connie Brown and Dorothy Killebrew also share stories of being called out to a new role.

In chapter 6, both Michael Alleman and Ruth Daugherty write about trials—those of Pharaoh and of modern-day United Methodists, respectively. Concluding Act II, in the midst of personal trials, Mary Merriman tells of receiving a literal (phone) call to a new ministerial role.

4

Growing Up
Exodus 2:11–22 and Hebrews 11:24–28

"MOSES GROWS UP"
BY ANDREA BROWN

I don't know about you, but this was not a part of the Moses story I learned in Sunday school. We jumped straight from the baby in the bulrushes to the burning bush. There was no murder in there. And it's not as if this story is just considered too PG-13; apparently, adults can't be trusted with it either. It's not in the lectionary, so churches that strictly follow that standard series of Bible lessons *never* hear this story preached. It seems like a cover up!

This is a pretty horrifying story. It doesn't go into detail, but take a moment to imagine it, if you will. It's messy, probably bloody, and definitely terrifying. Moses kills a man and buries him in the sand. That sandy burial part seems particularly creepy to me.

But you know what? It's July 4th weekend. Usually, around this holiday, I tell a story from American history in the sermon, and so I think I'll just do that today instead of talking about this whole Moses mess. That seems like a better idea than preaching on a scandalous story about a guy who is *supposed* to be one of our biblical heroes.

The story I'm going to tell you today is about William Parker. It's a very important story in American history and, in fact, in local history, even though most of us probably couldn't say who William Parker was. But the events I'm going to tell you about happened less than twenty miles from here. The year was 1851.

Parker was a mixed-race man. His mother, enslaved in Maryland, was of African descent; his father was probably white, so in some respects, he didn't totally belong in either culture. And even though some people probably thought of him as white and he might have been able to "pass," he chose to identify with other black people. And even after he himself was free, he continued to identify with and work for the good of those who remained enslaved.

And that kind of reminds me of Moses, actually, because he was brought up in two different cultures, and he chose to identify with his folks who were enslaved, not with his folks who were from the enslaving group. But, often, people didn't see him that way. One Hebrew guy said to him, "Who made you a ruler and judge over us?" (Exodus 2:14). To that guy, Moses must have looked like the palace brat he was; he must have looked like Pharaoh's grandson. Later on, when a bunch of Midianite girls were telling their father about meeting Moses, they said, "An Egyptian helped us" (Exodus 2:19). But, anyway, I'm not telling you about Moses today. I'm telling you about William Parker.

William Parker escaped from slavery in Maryland when he was seventeen. He ran over the Mason Dixon line into freedom in Pennsylvania. That was in 1838. He eventually married a woman named Eliza and they bought a house in Christiana, just south of Gap. They used it to help others move to freedom as part of the Underground Railroad. He organized a mutual protection society among black people in the area. Meanwhile, in 1849, four slaves ran away from another Maryland plantation—this one owned by Edward Gorsuch. I'm not proud to tell you that he was a Methodist Sunday School leader. These four men found their way to Parker's house.

Well, a year later, Congress passed the Fugitive Slave Act as part of the shameful Compromise of 1850, aimed at keeping the South from seceding. The Fugitive Slave Law allowed slave owners to "pursue and reclaim" escaped slaves across state lines using "such reasonable force and restraint as may be necessary, under the circumstances of the case, to take and remove such fugitive person back to the State or Territory whence he or she may have escaped" and—this was the especially galling part—a person attempting to "harbor or conceal such fugitive" could be subject to fine or imprisonment.[1] Residents of free states—white and black—were being required to cooperate with, and participate in, the slave system. (And, oh my gosh, that kind of reminds me of Pharaoh and the way he tried to force other people—Egyptian and Hebrew—to cooperate with his slave system. But I'm not talking about that story today.)

So in 1851, Gorsuch heard a rumor that his "property" was in Christiana. Following the laws of the day, he went to Philadelphia to obtain a federal warrant and the assistance of a deputy U.S. marshal. Gorsuch, his son, two friends, and Pharaoh (oops, I mean the federal marshal carrying a federal warrant) soon showed up on the Parkers's doorstep. But Parker had been tipped off by a member of his network who was working as a spy in the federal office where Gorsuch had gone for the warrant. So, when Gorsuch arrived, the four men he claimed to own, as well as the Parkers and some supporters, were waiting for them, barricaded on the second floor. The following is based on Vincent Harding's account.[2]

When the Sunday School leader burst in to the first floor, he yelled upstairs, "'I want my property.'" Parker called down: "'Go in the room down there, and see if there is anything belonging to you. There are beds and a bureau, chairs and other things. Then go out to the barn; there you will find a cow and some hogs. See if any of them are yours.'"

According to Harding, "At that point, the marshal began to talk of burning the house down. Hearing [that] suggestion, Parker's wife sounded a horn from the second-floor window, braving gunfire to do it." The horn was a signal to others in the area. Soon, about 100 black people and a handful of whites—four or five Quakers—arrived. When these folks learned that Gorsuch was a Methodist class leader, they began singing a Sunday School song to him, hoping to persuade him, morally and religiously, to leave: "Leader," they sang, "what do you say / About the judgment day?"

Still, he persisted and insisted on having his "property" back. Suddenly, guns were fired on both sides; it's impossible to say who fired first. But in the melee, Gorsuch "was beaten to the ground by one of the men he had come to reclaim." Then, "the women burst upon him."

As Vincent Harding poetically describes it, "They came leaping out of the rivers of Africa, urged up from the depths of the Atlantic, . . . [rising from the bellies of the slave ships], forcing their way out of the mourning

1. "Fugitive Slave Act 1850," sections 6 and 7.
2. Harding, *There Is a River*, 169–70.

grounds of the South." These were women (Jochebeds, you might say) who had seen their sons and daughters beaten and disrespected, who had themselves been victims of abuse of every kind at the hands of slave masters. They had had enough. They were not going to let one more son be taken back across the Nile River—I mean the Mason Dixon line. They "rushed from the house with corn cutters and scythe blades [and] hacked the bleeding and lifeless body" of Edward Gorsuch.[3]

Then Pharaoh came out in force. Forty-five U.S. Marines arrived. Before long, they had arrested some thirty-eight people on charges of high treason. But not William Parker. He escaped to Midian—I mean, to New York state.

Not one person was convicted in the case. (And by the way, Thaddeus Stevens, of Lancaster, was one of the defense attorneys working on behalf of the thirty-eight. If you remember the story we heard last week, you could say Stevens was playing the role of Pharaoh's daughter.) Not one person was convicted.

Among many challenges to the unjust Fugitive Slave Law, the Christiana Rebellion is considered the most significant in causing it to collapse. As Harding puts it, an end to slavery would not be won through academic discussions nor through the proscribed channels of law but through "personal, physical struggles to be free." Parker, fleeing North, was first sheltered by the abolitionist Frederick Douglass in Rochester, New York. At last he found a Promised Land in Canada.

I just can't help but talk about the Exodus story!

The fact is, Moses, like William Parker, is the sort of person we root for, even if we do not normally countenance violence. Moses is the twelve-year-old boy who, sick of seeing his little sister abused by their father, accidentally or intentionally kills the man to keep it from happening one more time. We do not blame him. Moses is a prisoner in a concentration camp who witnesses a fellow Jew being beaten and, without regard for personal consequences, slays the murderous Nazi. Moses doesn't turn himself in or face up to the consequences, which the story tells us would have been death by order of his affectionate, adoptive grandfather, Pharaoh. No, he runs away, and neither he nor the narrator of this story seems troubled by the killing—only by the risk that he might be caught.

---

3. Harding, 170, quoting H. U. Hensel, *The Christiana Riot* (Lancaster, PA: New Era, 1911), 33.

Why would God choose someone like *that* to lead the people to freedom? God sees that Moses is passionate, even to the point of stupidity, about protecting the oppressed. Not only does Moses strike the Egyptian he sees striking a Hebrew slave, he also calls out a Hebrew for striking a fellow Hebrew. He hates it when people are mistreated, no matter who is doing it. And he doesn't think much about his personal safety when such matters arise. When he sees some shepherds muscling out a bunch of young women at the well in Midian (and you can imagine the abusive language and other forms of harassment that might have accompanied that act), Moses takes up the girls' cause, even though he is thoroughly outnumbered. He has a gentleness to him despite his hot-headedness: a strong protective instinct and a wide streak of compassion.

According to biblical scholar Terence E. Fretheim, Moses "demonstrates a concern for . . . the life of the weaker members of the society, and an intolerance for abuse exercised by the strong."[4] Moses is like other third-culture kids—someone who doesn't totally *fit* in either of the cultures in which he was raised, yet can act as a bridge. Such people have very important roles to play. Fretheim also points out that "Moses's action anticipates . . . God's action." Both see, strike, and save. God and Moses *see* Israel's oppression, and by seeing it, we mean that it strikes a responsive chord in them; they are not indifferent to it but feel compelled to do something about it. Both *strike* Egyptians. Both *save* and deliver others from oppression and into freedom.[5]

In talking about the Exodus story up to this point, we've been thinking a lot about the role of ordinary Egyptians and Israelites. One of the lessons these stories have for ordinary Americans, and for Christians who happen to be Americans, on this Independence Day weekend has to do with the sneaky ways of Pharaoh. Political compromise can be one such sneaky tactic if used unjustly. While the ability to compromise is a good thing—and something that seems to be a lost art in our Congress—compromises can be used in the cause of justice or injustice.

In God's politics, the desire for unity never outranks the need for justice to be done. The Fugitive Slave Act of 1850 was an ungodly compromise that sought to co-opt good people in an evil system, for the sake of unity—keeping the peace at the expense of the people already most oppressed. Right now, some people in The United Methodist Church, in

4. Fretheim, *Exodus*, 45.

5. Fretheim, *Exodus*, 42–43.

order to prevent some particularly strident conservatives from seceding, are weighing whether to compromise on rights being demanded, justly, by gay and lesbian members.

We should weigh such proposals on the scales of history. Thursday marked the fiftieth anniversary of the signing of the Civil Rights Act of 1964. There is still work to be done to assure that all students—no matter what color their skin is or what neighborhood they come from—have the right to a quality education that gives them a fair chance to succeed. In some ways, we have slipped backwards in this regard. When society doesn't care for these matters through ordinary, peaceful channels, Moseses and William Parkers will eventually rise up. As Christians, we have a special responsibility to call out injustices in our country in order to protect the people God sees and saves.

REFLECTIONS BY RUTH A. DAUGHERTY

While the Searchers Class was studying the Bible, the Contemporary Issues Class met at the same time, focusing on current issues of injustice in society. Persons who were members of the Searchers Class sometimes attended the Contemporary Issues Class when there was an issue of particular interest to them, expressing the conflict of wanting to be in both classes. Thus, when the two classes were asked to consider merging into one, the response was positive. I was asked to continue leading the Bible study and to secure resource persons to give leadership when focusing on a particular issue. Most of all, it provided me the opportunity to grow in my relationship with God and my "neighbors," continuing the experiences I had on the Women's Division.

I remember that Theressa Hoover used to say that her morning devotions consisted of reading the Bible held in one hand and the *New York Times* in the other. It was her way of grounding herself in God's call on her life in the context of the current needs of society and the world. For her, the life of Jesus focused on our relationship with God and with one another—the summation of the law to love God and to love our neighbors and the Golden Rule to treat others as we want to be treated. Although Jesus attended the synagogue regularly, much of his time was spent walking through the towns and countryside, teaching and ministering to persons of diverse backgrounds. Jesus touched the untouchable; forgave without requiring retribution; accepted the unacceptable, included the excluded;

showed patience with disciples who were slow learners; did not tolerate the unjust practices of money changing in the temple; and said his disciples could do even greater things than he had done. Jesus spoke of persons appearing to be righteous but really being hypocrites (Matthew 23:28). This raised questions to be answered: How am I faithful to God in the way that Jesus taught and lived? Who are the people God calls us to relate to by following the model of Jesus's life?

Responding to these questions has led me to some meaningful though difficult experiences. I was arrested in Washington, DC, for demonstrating against South Africa's apartheid. I participated in a protest in Colorado against the production of nuclear bombs; led campaigns for writing letters to legislators for laws against discrimination; and trained persons to organize to bring about change for a peaceful, just society. And I worked to change discriminating laws of The United Methodist Church as a delegate to General Conference.

Therefore, when the Searchers Class and Contemporary Issues Class met as one, it seemed an opportunity to search the Bible for its relevancy for today in bringing about change in laws and practices that prevent persons from living the life abundant that Jesus proclaimed. As a result of the combined effort, the class began a study of homosexuality and the Bible.

Connie Brown has had the challenges of poverty and five school moves. She has also had many blessings, including nurturing by Evangelical United Brethren and United Methodist churches and Lebanon Valley College, where she met a mixture of people. She and her late husband, the Rev. Alan S. Brown, have a daughter, the Rev. Andrea Brown, and son Scott plus four grandchildren (including transgender and gay). Here, she describes receiving sexuality education at church in very indirect ways.

I can remember as a child of not more than seven years old, coming out of a little evangelical church in rural Pennsylvania, holding the hand of a little boy, the little brother of a friend of mine. A woman with a more man's-style haircut—and this would have been in the mid-1940s—the woman said to us, "Oh, hi kids, and whose little boy are you?" speaking directly to this child who was about three years of age. He said, "I'm Jimmy, and whose little boy are you?" And we all thought, "Hmmm. . .don't ask." This woman was well respected in this community, she lived alone. You knew her as an aunt of various people in this relatively small community. She even hired out to help with housework and things like that. But, you knew that there was something different about her.

We moved from there by the time I was eight years of age. There were a lot of moves, because my father, who had severe diabetes and mental illness, ended up in Harrisburg State Hospital. In those years, mental illness was something that you didn't talk about or mention to people.

Marjorie (Marge) Cumpston is a retired school librarian living in a retirement community in Lancaster. She is the mother of four daughters; two are gay and two are straight. Marge is a member of Grandview UMC and active in several gay-rights organizations. Here, she speaks about sexuality education at Grandview:

I think we need to get away from the either/or situation: sexual orientation is a continuum; it's not an either/or. On one side are a couple of people that will forever always be only attracted to those of the same sex. And over here there are a couple of people that will always be attracted to only people of the opposite sex. And then there's the rest of us that live in this great, wonderful mishegoss of the middle, and there are a few who live in the dead center of the middle, who are true bisexuals. But if you understand that that's a continuum, that it's not an either/or, it makes the whole situation much more likely, or probable, if you will. And I think that's critically important. And if you will listen to Andrea Brown teach sex education to our kids, that's what she talks about.

5

Encountering the Sacred
Exodus 2:23—4:23, 27–31

"HAVE YOU EVER STOOD ON HOLY GROUND?"
BY MICHAEL I. ALLEMAN

We continue the story of Exodus with Moses in exile. As you recall, the young-adult Moses had to leave his home after reacting to an Egyptian master beating an Israelite slave. Moses was furious. He looked around and, seeing no one, attacked the slave master. He *killed* the master and buried his body in the sand. But someone had witnessed what Moses had done, so he had to flee. Far from the land he had learned to call home, he is now married and has a child. We pick up the story with Moses in exile, shepherding his father-in-law Jethro's flock.

Moses by now is almost middle aged, working as a shepherd. We know that King David was a shepherd as a boy, and we remember from the story of Jacob that he sent his youngest son Joseph out to check on his other sons who were grazing the flocks. The sons were shepherds for their father. It's not a very prestigious job. And yet, in the midst of mundane shepherding, Moses finds himself standing on holy ground.

Have you ever found yourself standing on holy ground?

Moses took the flock out to the west side of the wilderness, Mt. Horeb or Mt. Sinai, both names for the same mountain. Mt. Sinai, you remember, is where God will give the Ten Commandments to Moses. That comes much later in the story. This time, an angel of God appears to Moses in a burning bush, a bush that's burning and yet not consumed. The figure is subtle, almost imperceptible. Some artists have portrayed this as a bush in flames, and in the midst of the flames, you can just barely make out an angel. We can imagine Moses turning to see the bush and thinking, "I'm gonna pay attention to this—I wonder if this is just a burning bush or whether there's more happening." Moses has the eyes to see that the bush is afire with God. He takes time to wonder, to pay attention, to consider if this bush has anything to do with him. Perhaps something more than just a bush is here. Moses says to himself, "I will turn aside and look at this bush." So, he turns aside and focuses on the bush, believing that, perhaps, there's more to it than fire.

When God sees that Moses is paying attention and listening, God calls from out of the bush, "Moses! Moses!" (Exodus 3:4). The God of all creation calls to one person! It always amazes me: the God of all that is, calls to us by name. I mean each one of us—it doesn't matter how old we are or how young we are, doesn't matter how learned, how slow, or how prestigious we are. Each of us, God calls by name, as if we were God's only child. It's so amazing.

Moses responds, "Here I am." We'll hear these words echoed as we keep reading Scriptures. When we get to the book of Samuel, we'll hear a story about a young boy in a temple whom God will call by name—"Samuel! Samuel!" And Samuel will reply, "Here I am" (1 Samuel 3:4–10). Moses is the first to respond this way.

"Do not come near—keep your distance," God warns. And at the same time, "Take off your shoes," he says. "Remove the sandals from your feet, for the place on which you are standing is holy ground" (Exodus 3:5).

Have you ever found yourself standing on holy ground? Imagine what it feels like, the hot sand under your feet. I remember very clearly what it feels like to stand on warm sand and to wiggle my toes and have the sand come up through my toes. I've just come from vacation, a week at the shore. The more I wiggle my toes and my feet, the deeper I begin to sink into the sand until the sand is surrounding me, the presence of this holy ground is embracing me and holding me and filling me. I believe the poet Elizabeth Barrett Browning has said it best: ". . . Earth's crammed with heaven, / And every common bush afire with God; / But only he who sees, takes off his shoes, / The rest sit round it and pluck blackberries . . . ."[1] We have to pay attention, to notice that the ground we stand on is holy—and then keep our distance.

God is telling Moses, "Keep your distance and yet enter into this intimate relationship with me." Both at the same time. "Don't let anything come between you and this holy ground. Remove your sandals so that your flesh will feel the holy ground beneath you. But not too close!"

Moses keeps his distance both physically and emotionally, filled with fear as we all might be, resisting what God is calling him to do. It kind of surprises me that Moses is so resistant to this call from God. Clearly, God's heart and Moses's heart are made from the same cloth. God says, "I've heard the cries of my people and I've come to their aid." Moses saw the plight of his people and struck out against the master, killing him, which is why he has ended up where he is today, shepherding sheep. Yet, he resists God's call. Five times he resists.

First Moses asks, "Who am I that you're sending? Who am I to go to speak to Pharaoh?" And God says, "I will be with you" (Exodus 3:11). "I am with the oppressed, with those who are slaves." I was in seminary the first time I heard that phrase—that God is on the side of the oppressed. I remember raising my hand and asking the professor, "Does that mean in order to be with God, I need to be oppressed?" My professor responded, "No, no, no! It *does* mean that if you want to be with God, you will be on the side of the oppressed."

Then, Moses responds, "Well, what is the name of the God who is calling me on such a dangerous task?" And God replies, "I AM WHO I AM" (Exodus 3:14). "I WILL BE WHAT I WILL BE." It is as if God is saying, "You will not tame me or contain me in a name. You will not determine who I am." This is the God-beyond-any-name that is calling to Moses. The one true God is calling for Moses to speak to Pharaoh on God's behalf. "I AM WHO I AM."

Third resistance. "What if they do not believe me?" God replies, "See that staff?" God says to Moses, "Throw it on the ground" (Exodus 4:2). Moses throws it down, and it becomes a serpent. Then God says, "Now pick it up by its tail." Moses picks it up by its tail, and it becomes a staff again. God now says, "Put your hand inside your cloak" (Exodus 4:6). Moses does so. When he removes it, it's white with leprosy. "Now put it back inside," God instructs. Moses puts it back inside, removes it, and now

1. Browning, "Aurora Leigh," 152.

it's healed. God continues: "And if that's not enough, then go down to the Nile, take some water out of the Nile, pour it on dry ground, and it will become blood."

But Moses protests again, claiming, "I do not speak well." God says, "Who created the mouth of man? Who created the dumb, the deaf, the blind, and those who can see? Did not the Lord your God create them? Can I not also put words into your mouth?" Finally, Moses blurts out, "But Lord, I don't want to do this. I just don't wanna do it. Get someone else to do it." At this, God becomes angry and says, "Your brother Aaron is already on his way to see you. I know Aaron has a fluid mouth. Aaron shall be your mouthpiece to Pharaoh and to the people. And you shall be for Aaron, God. You shall give my words to Aaron."

Now, we can come down pretty hard on Moses with all his excuses, trying to turn away from doing what God was calling him to. And yet, I think at one point or another we have to ask ourselves, "How would we respond if we were Moses?" Or maybe even a more personal question, "How have we responded in our own lives? Are we so different?" Consider this popular parable. You may have already seen it, but it makes a point about the risk of standing on holy ground.

One day, a woman noticed three older men with long white beards standing in her front yard. When she saw them, she thought they might be hungry and invited them inside to have something to eat. They replied, "Is your husband home?" "No," she said. They replied, "Then we cannot come in." Later, when her husband arrived home she went out again and said, "My husband is home, so come in and we'll give you something to eat." The men replied, "No, we cannot all enter the same home." "Why not?" she inquired. One man said, "Because that gentleman is Success and that gentleman is Wealth and my name is Love, and whenever any one of us enter the home, that home is filled with us. So, go in and talk with your husband and decide which one of us you would want to enter your home." The woman shared what she had just heard with her husband, who said, "This is great! Invite Wealth in, and the home will be filled with wealth!" But his wife replied, "Well, maybe we ought to invite Success in, and the home can be filled with success." Overhearing the conversation, their daughter jumped in and said, "No, no! You need to invite Love in because then our home will be filled with love." The husband and wife look at each other, exchanging glances that said, "Well, she has a point there, let's invite Love." So the woman went out again and asked, "Which one of you is Love?" Love raised his hand. "We invite you to come into our home." As Love began to move toward the door, so did Success and Wealth. Confused, the woman said, "I thought only one of you could enter into the home." The three men replied, "Wherever Love goes, Wealth and Success follow. So if you invite Love into your home, we all enter."

After reading that parable, I exclaimed out loud, "That just isn't true!" Consider Jesus—the very person who personified love, who came to live and proclaim the Word of God to us, was nailed to a cross. Now you might be able to say that, yes, his life was successful, but certainly you can't say his life was filled with wealth. The man didn't have two dimes to his name. Wealth does not always follow love. It just isn't true! We might want it to be true, but it just isn't true. Holy ground can be dangerous territory.

I think sometimes we want it to be true, that if God calls us, we will be safe and there will be no risk and no danger involved at all, but that's just not true. Moses knew Pharaoh. He *knew* the power that Pharaoh had and he *knew* that it would be dangerous to talk to him, with or without God's help. There's no kidding about that. He knew this was a dangerous calling. He had no illusion about the risk of God's call, and I hope none of us have illusions either when we find ourselves standing on holy ground.

God calls us to keep our distance yet, at the same time, to take off our shoes and have this intimate relationship with God. The only way to do that is to make ourselves vulnerable, and being vulnerable is about showing up and being willing to be seen. Responding to God's call is not about controlling. It is not about knowing. It's about the vulnerability of belief and trust. It is about showing up and being willing to be seen for who you are. Ultimately, I join Moses in saying, "Here am I. Okay, God, I will go where you've called me. And, Lord, I will strive to trust that you have called me because, with you, I believe I am enough."

Have you ever stood on holy ground?

Have you ever stood before the altar and made a promise to someone that you will be with them, that your very life will be with them always even though you have no idea what awaits you in the future?

Have you ever had the wife of your friend die and you know that you need to go see your friend, but the last thing you want to do is go see your friend, because you're not good at this stuff. You don't know what to say, you're awkward. You know it's just not your thing. And you begin to rationalize in your mind—they probably really just want to be with their own family, so you find things to keep you from going—but what you really need to do is to go be with your friend. So you force yourself to get into the car. You force yourself to start the car, put it into gear, and drive to your friend's home. You force yourself to get out and to walk up the walk and press the doorbell. And your friend opens the door and says, "I knew you would come." You spend fifteen, twenty minutes with him and you are terrible at this. You don't say the right things, you know you aren't saying the right things. You're crying when you're trying to be strong for him. You leave after twenty minutes and you're going to your car thinking, "What did I say? I'm sure I was of no value to him at all." And a week later, you get this note in the mail that says, "You don't even know how much that visit meant to me. It helped me to get through it."

Love is an action verb. It takes courage. It was Theodore Roosevelt who said,

> It is not the critic who counts; not the man who points out how the strong man stumbles, or where the doer of deeds could have done them better. The credit belongs to the man who is actually in the arena, whose face is marred by dust and sweat and blood; who strives valiantly; who errs, who comes short again and again, because there is no effort without error and shortcoming; but who does actually strive to do the deeds; who knows great enthusiasms, the great devotions; who spends himself in a worthy cause; who at the best knows in the end the triumph of high achievement, and who at the worst, if he fails, at least fails while daring greatly . . . ."[2]

Standing on holy ground means taking a risk for God.

Have you ever stood on holy ground?—when you knew something had to be done and God was calling you to do it, and you were willing to dare greatly? When you stepped into the ring to be seen, believing that you are not alone, but that God was with you, and that somehow if God was with you, in your midst, it would be enough? I can only imagine that's how Moses must have felt. I can only imagine that's how he felt, standing on holy ground.

REFLECTIONS BY RUTH A. DAUGHERTY

I have experienced God working in my life at unexpected places. One of those places was the church parking lot at Mount Gretna United Methodist Church. After an event at the church, a United Methodist woman

2. Roosevelt, "Citizenship in a Republic."

approached and asked to speak with me as I was going to my car. She began by noting her respect for my opinions because I usually had good rationales for the positions taken on issues in the Women's Division. However, she was puzzled by my opposing the full rights of homosexuals to be ordained when I had expressed belief that all are created and loved by God. She asked me to share my reasons. I began by talking about the high calling to ministry and the set-apartness of ordination that, for me, entailed not only preaching and teaching God's word but also being an example in lifestyle. She asked me to share my thoughts about why God would not call homosexuals to a life committed to Christian ministry. After several attempts to explain my position, I became aware that what I was saying did not make sense—even to me. I thanked her for her concern and promised to give the matter more thought.

That event became a turning point in my life not only in changing my views but also how I dealt with persons who differed from me on issues. I determined to respect the views of others with whom I disagreed and sincerely ask questions to understand their views. That ordinary church parking lot became holy ground where I believe God spoke through a friend to challenge me in a manner that changed my understanding and led me to a commitment to be an advocate for full rights for all persons in our church.

Connie Brown: We joined a church in the Harrisburg suburbs when we eventually moved there, a small Evangelical United Brethren congregation, again. We had a young pastor, relatively new, just as we were relatively new. The people in the congregation were saying, Oh, Reverend Snyder's a nice-looking fellow; I've got to introduce him to my daughter, my niece, etc. Eventually he married a young woman from the community. He would preach beautiful sermons, and sometimes they included stories from his family life with his wife and young son.

They were wonderfully nurturing to the whole congregation, loved and respected, and made sure there were good confirmation and Bible school classes, plus scholarship money for kids to go to camp (I was one of those who had the privilege of that). He took the church out to explore and learn about things in Philadelphia, Washington, etc., and this was now the mid 1950s, when not too many congregations were venturing to do this. He was there to help my mother find a job when she lost hers; and now widowed, this is vitally important. So he was just subtly there for our family, and there were stories from so many families in the congregation of Reverend Snyder's helpfulness.

But, by 1959, after my mother had also died, my stepfather picked me up from college and said, "Guess what the big news is in the community? Reverend Snyder is gay." And of course the church is shocked and upset, and all the fellows who had gone hunting with him said, "Well, I'm never going hunting with him anymore." Same man he's always been, but there was all this terrible rejection. He could no longer be a pastor—this man who had been so caring and wonderful. I went with Alan, the nice young man whom I had met in high school and was dating, to visit at Rev. Snyder's home. He was very guarded. You know, I think he was thankful we came but very, very guarded because he had been hurt so much by the community.

Dorothy Hickok Killebrew was raised on a dairy and poultry farm and earned a BS in Agriculture Education from Penn State University prior to serving as an agricultural missionary in Zimbabwe for four and a half years. She and her late husband, Milton, both served as pastors of various United Methodist churches in the Susquehanna Conference in Pennsylvania. She is now married to Bob Neuhauser and is active at Grandview UMC.

When I was a pastor in Altoona, my husband was approached to lead a Bible study with the gay community. Actually, what ended up was they led it and I learned a lot. The Bible study met from 1:30–4 p.m. on Saturday and Sunday afternoons. My husband said, "Wow, if we'd had interest in Bible study like that in the church!" And as a pastor appointed to Lewistown, I found sometimes there were church members who didn't even come to my Bible studies because I was a woman.

Sometime later, a couple of the gay people who attended my congregation approached me that their friend in Clearfield had died. They were concerned that there was no pastor in Clearfield for them . . . they didn't feel comfortable. They didn't know who they could approach. So I went to Clearfield to officiate at the funeral. This was the first time that I officiated at a funeral where people did not know the 23rd Psalm; they didn't know the Lord's Prayer. They were really not church-attending people, largely because of how they were not accepted.

The siblings of the person who died wanted to take the house from his spouse. The one who prevented it was their father, who lived in a nursing home. The only ones who ever came to visit him were this male couple. It was incredible.

6

Trials
Exodus, chapters 5–11

"HARD-HEARTED PHARAOH AND THE PLAGUES"
BY MICHAEL I. ALLEMAN

What are we to make of this story about the plagues? How is God's grace shown through the hard-hearted Pharaoh? It's not easy to find grace in this story.

The first thing that jumped out at me was the power of God through these plagues. God is the all-powerful being able to do such things. People who have found themselves in the midst of terrible storms have talked about this awesome power released. We recognize the power of God just listening to these plagues being revealed to us. The story also reveals to us the skewed image that Pharaoh has of himself and his own power. Remember, five different times, God has Pharaoh on his knees crying uncle. "Okay, okay, you win. I give up. Just take these plagues away from me." And five different times, God does stop the plague. Pharaoh gets up and changes his mind and does not release the people. Five different times.

Some have suggested that Pharaoh's thoughts are a little psychotic. Pharaoh looks at the God who brings him to his knees and to whom he cries uncle, then changes his mind and says he is much more powerful than this God. Let's think about this. When I pretend that there's something in my life that I don't really want to share with God or when I'm trying to keep a secret from God or when I think I can depend on my own power without God's help, even I'd describe my thoughts as psychotic. So maybe the suggestion that Pharaoh's thoughts are somewhat psychotic is worth consideration. After all, we are trying to fool the God of all creation who knows all!

The next thing that strikes me is that, from the reading, we hear that Moses is eighty years old and Aaron is eighty-three. That's funny, because in my mind I always have Aaron as being the younger brother. After all, Aaron is the mouthpiece. It is Moses who tells him what to say. I could see a younger brother doing that. But an older brother? An older brother speaking as if the words from Moses are God's words? Wow that's really something. And I suspect that these words have hit me harder because a year from now I retire at age sixty-two, and when I hear that Aaron was eighty-three and Moses was eighty, I think, "Well, maybe I still have twenty years here where God can use me." It's a heart-rending thing for me to think about.

I think for the church—not only our congregation but also the church at large—there has never been a time in our lives, in our history, when retired people have been healthier than they are now. Which means we have this whole resource of people to be in ministry and mission that years ago we didn't have. These days retirement is going to look a little different. We have to recognize that with retirement comes freedom—people have waited their whole lives to do certain things and now have the freedom to do it. So, in the church we might be seeing teams of two and three people working together to cover a task previously covered by one person. They can help each other when one has to go there, go here, whatever. We need to think about the ministry and mission that can happen with these thriving retirees as we move forward. I just pray that we make use of this newfound resource, allowing the world to see the hands and feet and voice of Christ in our retired folks more fully than ever before.

The third thing that struck my mind was that Moses goes to Pharaoh to plead for Pharaoh to let his people go and when he does, you remember Pharaoh's response: not only "no" but also, "Well, if you have this much energy, then you're not just going to make as many bricks as you did before, but rather than have the straw delivered to you, you'll be expected to gather the straw, too. Yes, collect the straw as well as make just as many bricks as before." And when the Israelites hear this, they respond to Moses saying,

"The Lord look upon you and judge! You have brought us into bad odor with Pharaoh and his officials, and have put a sword in their hand to kill us" (Exodus 5:21). As if it's Moses's fault. Are they forgetting that it's their cries, their tears that got God's attention long before this? The most that Moses did was reveal how hard-hearted Pharaoh really is.

Whenever we look at any oppression, we realize that once it is brought out into the light, it can't be shoved back into the darkness. We can't pretend it doesn't exist. We can't ignore it. Once it is brought into the light we have to deal with it. And we know that as difficult as it is, the only way forward is through it. Trust me, I understand those first few steps in fighting oppression are so very painful by those who are being oppressed. Always is. Powerful people don't want to let go. They're winning here. They're afraid of what they'll lose if things change. These are very, very difficult first steps.

But what I really want to focus on in this passage is that no less than a dozen times, this Scripture says to us that God hardened the heart of Pharaoh. God revealed Pharaoh's hardened heart. I want to ask this question: "Which is it here? That Pharaoh is this pawn, this poor victim whose heart is hardened by God? That he has no control, since God is the one doing this, hardening Pharaoh's heart? Or is it that God is revealing Pharaoh's hardened heart?" Five times, five times, Pharaoh says, "I give; I give. Just stop the plague, and I'll let the people go." And five times, God stops the plague. And five times, Pharaoh changes his mind and doesn't let the Israelites go. What's that old saying: "Fool me once, shame on you. Fool me twice, shame on me." The whole image is that to be fooled once reflects the nature of someone else. But if I know that person's nature, and I still continue to be fooled over and over, then it's me. So, we look at God and say, "What is this? Is God being fooled five times?" Or, is God saying to Pharaoh over and over again, "Here's your chance to turn around and head in a new direction, to open your heart just a little bit, to change who you are." And five times, Pharaoh says, "No thanks; no thanks. I'll just remain who I am."

I think there's a huge, huge difference between someone who doesn't know any better and someone who intentionally tries to destroy someone's life. If you remember the movie *Good Morning Vietnam*, you'll recall Robin Williams's character. And if you know anything about the late Robin Williams, you know he had no filter at all. So anything that came into Robin Williams's mind came out of his mouth. And that's pretty much the role that he plays in this film. He plays a DJ, Adrian Cronauer, for the radio station in Vietnam for all the soldiers to hear, and everything comes out;

there's just no filter at all. Truth is coming out; humor is coming out. He's playing songs that they remember from back home and there's this whole new sense of hope and vitality being brought back to the soldiers. The general loves Cronauer, but his direct supervisor does not like him and wants to get rid of him. In fact, he wants to destroy him. So much so that when Cronauer is on leave, his supervisor directs him to go on a road that is known to be not just a dangerous road but also a road that is occupied by the enemy. The Jeep gets hit with a shell and they survive. But when they return, Cronauer's supervisor is not finished with him. Now he paints the picture that Robin Williams's character is conversing with the enemy, forcing him to be dishonorably discharged and shipped back to the states, no longer a DJ. What I love about this piece in the movie is when the general talks to his supervisor. The general says, "Dick, I've covered for you a lot of times, 'cause I thought you was a little crazy. But you're not crazy, you're mean." Not crazy or psychotic, just mean.

Pharaoh is like that. I don't think Pharaoh is psychotic; I think he's just mean. Mean-spirited. Hard-hearted. More interested in keeping his power over other people than lifting a finger to help anyone else. So I want to ask the question, "What is it that makes Pharaoh's heart so hard and does not allow the Israelites to have a hard heart, but an open heart? What is it that makes that happen?" I know power corrupts. Absolute power corrupts absolutely. But more importantly, Pharaoh doesn't believe he needs help from anyone else at all. Not even God. Pharaoh has all the power; he thinks he needs no one else. Nothing hardens a heart more quickly than the notion that I don't need anyone else's help, that I can do this on my own, lift myself up by my own bootstraps. I can take care of myself; I don't need anyone else.

We can hear the lie in this attitude all through Jesus's preaching, over and over again in the parables he taught. Consider the parable of the prodigal son—he was telling this parable in the midst of the Pharisees and Scribes, those who knew the law best (Luke 15:11–32). It goes something like this: A father has two sons. The younger of the sons demands his portion of the inheritance, which is to say, "I wish you were dead, Dad." Then he goes, spends that money frivolously, and realizes he was better off at home than on his own. So, he comes back, and while he is still a far distance, his father sees him and runs out, throws his arms around him and says, "This is my son who was dead and is now alive. Come let's kill the fatted calf for him." He hasn't done a thing to earn his father's love. "No, this is my son whom I love." The eldest brother is out in the field and says, "I've been here all along and now here's this younger brother who has done everything wrong." And the father says to the older brother, "I've always loved you, not because of what you've done but because you're my son."

Consider the parable of the Good Samaritan (Luke 10:25–37). A man was traveling from Jericho to Jerusalem, falls among thieves who rob him and leave him half dead. While he's lying there, the good Jewish people come and go by the side—for good reason: so they don't become unclean by touching him as the laws say they would become. Then a Samaritan, a lowly Samaritan, comes by and sees the man and reaches out to help him, treating his wounds, putting him on his own donkey, and taking him to the inn and caring for him there. He has the innkeeper take care of him and give him the bill, whatever the cost. Then Jesus turns to the listeners and asks them, "Who proved to be neighbor to this man?" They all say, "Why, the Samaritan." Jesus replies, "That's right. Go and do likewise. Go and be like that Samaritan. Go, and when you're lying there in need of help, allow a Samaritan to help you." For the powerful, this parable hits home.

Don't insist on going it alone, by your own power. Allow the gift of God's unmerited grace to enter your life. When we remind ourselves over and over again that none of us earns God's love, that it's always a gift given to us, a gift that we so desperately need, that whenever we receive it, it has the power to transform our lives. When we know that we need the help of others and we need the help of God. Whenever we see someone else then, it's such a small step for us to put ourselves into the shoes of someone who is in need because we're in need every day of our lives. We know what it feels like to be in need. So we can more easily put ourselves into the shoes of someone else in need. I think Pharaoh had the opportunity over and over and over again to change his hard heart. And he chose not to.

Calvin Miller wrote a trilogy—*The Singer, The Song,* and *The Finale.* These are marvelous, marvelous little books. In his book *The Singer,* Miller, as Pilgrim says, "God, can you be merciful and send me off to hell and lock me in forever?" God replies, "No, Pilgrim, I will not send you there, but if you chose to go there, I could never lock you out."[1]

When we know ourselves as ones who stand in need of God's grace and help, our hearts are so much more open, not only to God, but to everyone else as well. That's the best remedy that I know of—to have an open heart. To have a soft heart. To have a heart that is able to give to others. And to receive.

1. Miller, *The Singer Trilogy,* 135.

REFLECTIONS BY RUTH A. DAUGHERTY

Hope! That word has been a mantra for me while involved in the struggles for justice and especially for the elimination of the persecution and lack of full rights for LGBTQIA+ persons. That word became meaningful to me as I searched the Scriptures to understand how God persisted in various ways to change the self-centered, destructive, alienating, unfaithful, ungrateful ways of humanity. Then I read Paul's reference to God in his prayer in Romans 15:13, "May the God of hope fill you with all joy and peace in believing, so that you may abound in hope by the power of the Holy Spirit."

I believe the power of the Holy Spirit continues to undergird me with hope even when actions for change are rebuffed. I remember the times in the Bible that it was persistence after a number of attempts that brought the final sought-after results. Through the years, there have been opportunities to advocate for inclusiveness, particularly of LGBTQIA+ persons. Many of these involved me personally. Some that are vivid memories are:

Trial of Beth Stroud. She was an ordained UMC clergywoman who acknowledged in a sermon at First UMC of Germantown that she was a "self-avowed practicing" lesbian (to use the language of UMC church law) and was charged with violation of the United Methodist *Discipline*. Her trial was held at Camp Innabah in 2003. I joined a group of protesters and helped to hold a sign that read, "Love Not Law." Later, as I thought about that sign, I wondered if it should have said, "Love is the Law," based upon the answer given to Jesus when asked about the greatest commandment and his response to love God and neighbor. The ordination credentials of Beth Stroud were removed. An appeal was made, but the verdict of the trial was upheld.

General Conference of the UMC in 2004. During a plenary session, I made a motion to change the wording in the Social Principles to state that *some* members believe the practice of homosexuality is incompatible with Christian teaching. The motion was only narrowly defeated. To me, that was encouraging because the motion was made without prior knowledge of any groups advocating for or against the present language in the Social Principles. This indicated to me that when delegates voted on a motion without discussion with or pressure from organized groups, there was more likelihood of making some changes

Embrace. An inter-faith group in Lancaster committed to working for full inclusion of LGBTQIA+ persons in faith communities asked me to be the chair in 2012. I accepted and have been working with representatives of several faith communities to provide educational events such as showing DVDs of true stories of LGBTQIA+ persons, giving DVDs to the library for circulation, participating in annual PRIDE events, and working with other organizations for full inclusion. Several churches in the Lancaster area have become Welcoming Congregations.

Trial of Frank Schaefer. Frank Schaefer, ordained UMC clergy, performed the wedding of his son and his partner, which is a chargeable act in the UMC *Discipline.* A trial was held in November 2013 at Camp Innabah. I joined the protesters and attended the lengthy proceedings. The jury brought the verdict of guilty and requested him to promise he would not perform any marriage ceremonies for gay or lesbian couples in the future and gave him thirty days to respond to the conference Board of Ordained Ministry. If he refused to make that commitment, his ordination credentials would be removed. Frank Schaefer stated he was called to minister to all people and refused to make that promise. His credentials were removed, but he appealed to the Northeastern Jurisdiction Committee on Appeals, which reinstated his credentials.[2]

Wedding of Gay Couple. Gay members of Arch Street UMC in Philadelphia were married in that church on October 3, 2014, with more than fifty UMC clergy officiating. The event was significant to the life of the church. Charges were brought against thirty-six of the clergy who were members of the Eastern Pennsylvania Conference. The bishop met with all parties involved in the charges, and resolution was made. Those charged acknowledged violation of the rules of the UMC *Discipline,* and the two parties agreed to meet twice to dialogue about the issues of disagreement and the role of the *Discipline* in their life together.

Motion to Delete. At the 2015 Eastern Pennsylvania (EPA) Annual Conference, a resolution was made, "Affirming our Covenant and Accountability." I made a motion to delete the part, "Be it Further Resolved that the EPA Conference calls upon those clergy who feel they can no longer abide by our common covenant to withdraw themselves from our connection, rather than to continue to cause damage to our ministry through ongoing judicial proceedings." My motion was defeated.

In spite of the refusal of those in power in determining the rules of the church, I have hope that there will be action that will bring the end of discrimination in The United Methodist Church so the oppressed can truly experience freedom.

2. Schaefer, http://franklynschaefer.com.

TESTIMONY BY MARY MERRIMAN

In early 1987, I felt a need to leave Good News MCC. I was emotionally drained following my dad's death as well as living with a constant fear of the potential that our foster babies might also die from AIDS. I was exhausted from providing full-time care for the babies while Jan worked closing modular homes. When Jan got home, I would work for the church while she cared for the babies.

One morning about 3 a.m., having resigned as pastor of Good News MCC, I was sitting in a rocking chair feeding Gail. A TV evangelist told a story about a marginally employed, poor pastor with little food and support, who received a phone call one day inviting him to become an associate pastor in a church several states away. The story touched my heart, and I sobbed in prayer, "Please God, I know I need to get back to ministry but please couldn't you make this easy and just give me a phone call to the church you want me to serve?" The next day, I received a call from Adam DeBaugh, District Coordinator of the Mid-Atlantic District of MCC, inviting me to become the pastor of Vision of Hope MCC in Lancaster, Pennsylvania—a congregation of eleven people!

While I was blessed by this phone call, we also faced many challenges that would make this transition difficult. Jan was uncertain about leaving Florida, as she had not yet discerned God's call for her to go to Lancaster. The Polk County Florida Children and Youth Agency was uncertain about what to do with the babies, as they still had not found homes for children with AIDS in Central and Northern Florida. I was uncertain because the salary was a stipend of $600 a month—the same salary I had left at Lakeland. The state of Florida would have to agree to let the children relocate to Pennsylvania, and Pennsylvania would have to agree to provide adequate support as well. In the end, God moved the mountains! One prayer after the next was answered.

Both blessings and challenges would characterize the next few years of our ministry and family life. Our daughters grew strong physically, emotionally, and spiritually in the midst of our new community of faith at MCC and the Mid-Atlantic District. The church experienced significant growth, requiring additional time and energy from both me and Jan. We grew farther apart. By 1988, science learned that many babies diagnosed with HIV/AIDS were sero-converting to a diagnosis of HIV negative, as happened for Marie and Gail. This opened new family possibilities for both of them. Marie was eligible for adoption, and a forever family opened their home and hearts to her. Initially fearful of the HIV virus and cocaine addiction, Gail's grandmother now felt that it was time for Gail to return to live with her grandmother, father, and her siblings. Both girls returned to Florida. In the midst of these and other changes, Jan and I decided to go our separate ways. Two years later, I met the woman whom I would one day marry.

ACT III

Coming Out with a New Identity

"Families from the congregation, who were already well-known, were willing to sit in a Sunday School class . . . and [they] brought pictures of their entire families and said, 'Can you tell which ones are gay or straight?' And they just told us their life stories. People began to realize, oh, we've had gay people in the church forever."

—Connie Brown, on Grandview's process of discernment

"Mom, neither my home nor my church ever told me anything was wrong [with me]."

—gay daughter of Marge Cumpston,
on why their family never had a "coming-out" story

Coming out is an irreversible entry into a new public identity. There's really no way to recover the secret; there's no going back. For better or worse, the world will thereafter be a different place and me a different person in it. Coming out is a process of publicly embracing the identity you've always had but in many cases did not fully know yourself.

One of my college roommates came out as gay two years after we graduated. Paul had told his family during his sophomore year, but his brothers and sisters were not ready to hear it. His parents, he said, were very supportive though they couldn't pretend to understand what he was going through. They thought it was a "phase"—something he needed to work through while in college. Apparently, there was a lot of denial. This probably contributed to his hesitancy to come out to friends in college. When he finally did tell me, I was happy for him, at last free to be fully who he is, even if I was a bit perplexed about how he could have kept this from me for so many years. He waited until medical school to come out to his friends, and I can't blame him.

Our college was socially liberal but still proved a threatening atmosphere for gay people. The gay student club had a group picture in the yearbook in which all the members covered their faces. They wanted their existence to be known but didn't want people to identify them individually. The social climate was poisonous. No shortage of anti-gay verbiage came out of my mouth and those of my peers, oblivious as we were to how it sounded or what effect it might have on Paul and others like him. In the mid-1980s, the word "gay" was a common slur and "faggot" a popular insult. It didn't really occur to me that these words had personal meaning and that my friend would be wounded each time I uttered them.

At about the same point in my life, I was very involved in church and sang with a prominent church choir that toured regularly. This congregation was very welcoming to gays and lesbians, but it would be another decade before they would be ready to include a printed statement of welcome and inclusion in their bulletin. After two years in the choir, another college friend—she sang soprano in the choir—pointed out to me that I was the only unmarried, straight guy in the choir. I was incredulous! I knew a couple of the tenors were gay but had no idea about the others. Really? This was something of a coming out for me, as a heterosexual—a newfound awareness of my own sexuality in relation to others around me.

*　　*　　*

Sometimes coming out can feel like being kicked out, or jettisoned into a new place. Flashback about fifteen years earlier. After my parents got divorced, my mother moved my younger brother and me from Largo, Florida, to Atlanta, Georgia, her hometown. We were near both sets of grandparents and many aunts and uncles, so this was good. But the experience of crossing this sea of change left me angry and confused. The divorce of one's parents is a life-altering event. There was no going back to the way things were before. I entered a new school halfway through second grade. We searched for a new church community. We lived in an impersonal apartment. I had a new identity—a child of a broken family.

Somewhere in the midst of this chaos, I received a package in the mail. It was a Bible with my name on it, from Anona United Methodist Church in Largo, Florida, the church we used to belong to before the move. I was now in third grade, and they had sent me my third-grade bible, even though we no longer attended that congregation. Even at this young age, I recognized the grace of God in this community's thoughtfulness. Anona UMC taught me the power of a community's love. I don't want to make them out as saints; none of us are. I learned years later that they were not kind to my father, whom they blamed for the failed marriage. Methodists had taught against the sin of divorce for nearly a century. Divorce was the quintessential moral failing in Methodism, and people took sides. Despite this community's harsh moral judgment, they succeeded in being a vessel of God's grace when I needed them most. Even at this young age, I knew that my identity was wrapped up in Christian community.

*   *   *

In the story of Exodus, God prepares the Israelites for a departure from Egypt that will solidify their identity as the people of God, though it will still take them a while to accept this identity and understand what that means for their relationship with God. The Passover is a defining event, marking the Hebrews as God's chosen in distinction from the Egyptians. The crossing of the Sea of Reeds is another defining event, a way out of Egypt that can never be reversed. There is terrible carnage in both events. Must a coming out be so violent? Through both events, the Israelites become more fully aware of themselves as the people of God, set apart by God with this special identity.

In Act III, "coming out" takes on many forms and identities. In chapter 7, "Blood of Sacrifice," Michael Alleman preaches about the Passover story, relating this blood sacrifice to the sacrifice of Christ. Ruth Daugherty writes about some of the relationships at Grandview that prompted this congregation to come out in support of gay and lesbian people and to journey with them in ministry. Grandview member Marge Cumpston shares her family's story and her experience with PFLAG. Mary Merriman concludes this chapter, telling about living a closeted life and then coming out to her biological family and facing rejection.

Chapter 8, "Committing to the Journey," is about moving forward with a new identity. In her sermon, "The Journey Out," Andrea Brown proclaims hope in God, who makes a way *when there is no way*, based on the story of the Hebrews crossing the Sea of Reeds. In reflection, Ruth Daugherty tells the sequence of events as Grandview crossed over a sea of social change to become a Reconciling Congregation. Then, Connie Brown, Lou Cumpston, and Andrea Brown each share reflections and remembrances related to coming out, including Andrea's transgender niece Kate's visit to Grandview. This act concludes with Mary Merriman's work for civil rights in Lancaster County. She shares testimony about Vision of Hope MCC's struggle and eventual success, through intentional relationship-building and lots of prayer, in buying its first church property amidst threats of violence.

7

Blood of Sacrifice
Exodus 12:1–36

"PASSOVER & KILLING OF THE FIRSTBORN"
BY MICHAEL I. ALLEMAN

Every time we come back to the Exodus story, it seems, we start out saying, "Oh, this is an extremely important part of the Exodus story." I start out with the same words this time. This is an extremely important part of the Exodus story. We've said it before when the Hebrew midwives defied Pharaoh's order that they kill any newborn Hebrew boy. Because of their defiance, Moses lived. Then we said it when Moses saw the burning bush and heard God's calling out of that burning bush. Then we said it when nine different plagues came to Egypt and the people of Egypt, each time Pharaoh's heart growing harder. And we say it again with the arrival of the tenth plague, the Passover, and the angel of death. Now I ask you, "Which one of these is not an important piece in the Exodus story?" They are all important pieces.

In this sermon, we focus on the Passover, God's call to the Hebrew people to prepare for the angel of death to pass over their homes. They're told to sacrifice a lamb, to take the blood, capture it in a bowl, and to take a hyssop and put it on the mantel, the top frame of the door as a mark there.

They're told to mark both sides of the frame of the door, on either side, so that the angel of death will pass over their home.

There are two things that I want us to be aware of before we go any further in this story: one is that I believe that this is a Hebrew story. This is a Jewish story. I want to honor that; I don't want to make this Passover story anything that it's not. It stands on its own as a Jewish story. And while I believe that as a Christian, I can put a whole layer of meaning on top of it, it still remains for me primarily a Jewish story. And that's a good thing. It's important for us to remember that Jesus was a Jew. He didn't just happen to be a Jew; it was essential that he was a Jew. It was from the Jewish people that the Messiah would rise up. It was important that Jesus was girded in this understanding of the God of all creation. So that's important for us to remember and keep hold of.

The second thing I want to make a disclaimer on: when we hear this story of the angel of death falling on the homes of the people of Egypt, it's not a "Rah, rah, rah, yes! Pharaoh got what was coming to him!" moment. No, no, no. Listen to the story. All of Egypt cried out. Everyone—from Pharaoh to the people who worked under Pharaoh to every person in prison—was crying out with pain because there was a loss in their household. Not just any loss but the loss of their first-born child.

My four-year-old grandson Luke was reading with his father, my son Matt, the storybook by Bishop Tutu that we give to all of our baptized children. As they were reading through this Bible storybook, they just happened to be at Exodus and they just happened to be reading about the Passover. And if that's not bad enough, there's a picture in the book of Pharaoh standing there with his limp, dead child in his arms. Four-year old Luke became frightened and turned to his Daddy and said, "Daddy, will the angel of death come for me some night?" And he said, "No, no." Luke then asked, "The children who died—did they go to Heaven? What's it like, do you go up to Heaven or do you go through a door to Heaven?" And of course, in this age of marvelous technology and instant messaging, all of these questions came to land at Grandpa's feet to answer. How should I respond?

Sometimes a story like that will trigger unrelated questions and thoughts and images in our own minds. It's times like this that I yearn to be closer to my grandkids, who all live a full day's drive from here. Eight and a half hours to Detroit, Michigan, eight and a half hours to almost Charlotte, North Carolina. If I had been there, I would have grabbed Luke in my arms and said, "Ah, Luke this is a scary story, isn't it? And no, no, no, Luke, God did not want to kill these children. God tried very hard—nine times, God sent a plague to Pharaoh to try and change Pharaoh's heart so that the children would not die. God tried everything God knew how to do to change Pharaoh's heart so that these children would not have to die."

It's my understanding that the Jewish people, whenever they're celebrating the Passover feast and they get to this moment, when the angel of death enters into the homes of the Egyptians and kills the first-born male, that it is remembered very solemnly. It's always remembered in the context that these Egyptian people were also children of God. It's a great reminder to us that God creates all people in the image of God, starting with Adam and Eve. From that time and place, people have traveled here and there, all around the world, so we are now people of different colors of skin, different cultures, different languages, and different nationalities. When we remember this history, we so often remember it backwards. We start with all the differences and so often can't get past that to get back to the truth that we are all created in the image of God. We just get it backwards. Sometimes we get to the "all of us" but most often we never get there. Never get there.

Rob Bell is a pastor who began a church in Michigan, Mars Hills Bible Church. Very successful—it grew to over 10,000 members. And I think now, Bell lives in northern California, but at any rate, he was very effective as a pastor in this community church. I remember two stories about his ministry. A number of years ago, as I recall the story, he was sitting at a round table with people that he didn't know, and they were getting to know each other by sharing a little bit about what they did, experiences, where they'd been in their lives. As they were going around, one man said he was an ex-Marine. He had been in the first wave that went into the Gulf War in 1991. He said what a bizarre experience that was and what a bizarre experience the whole war was, the whole fighting was, for him. He talked about entering into enemy territory where bullets were flying, people were shooting at him. Shortly after that, they had an encounter with the enemy that they quickly won and had to put them in handcuffs. They lined them up, trying to put the handcuffs on them, when one man came running up and said, "You need to mail this, you need to mail this letter for me," just disrupting everything. This prisoner of war got in his face demanding, "You need to mail this letter for me so that my father knows that I love him." Looking around the table at Rob and the others, this ex-Marine remarked, "That man had no way of knowing how estranged I was from my father. So here I am in a foreign land, in a desert, in Iraq, bullets flying at me, having to now put handcuffs on the very people that were shooting at me, and I realize I could be that man."

I also remember another story about Bell. As I remember it told, a woman called his church and said she needed to talk with him. When she arrived for her appointment, he asked, "How can I help you?" She replied, "Well, I'm a prostitute, and I just can't do this anymore. I'm going to take my own life." And then she continued by sharing with him exactly how she was going to do it, where she was going to do it, and when she was going to do it. She said, "What I need from you is to know whether I will go to Heaven or hell when I die." Bell said that in the midst of sharing all of the information with him, she had mentioned something about a daughter who she had because one of her clients got her pregnant, and she was sure that the family would take care of the daughter. He asked her to say a little bit more about the daughter, and she did, and then he said, "What's the name of your daughter?" And she said, "The name of my daughter is Faith."

There are moments when the enemy is just like us. There are moments when they are us, those people are who we are, he is me, she is me. As much as we want to try and divide people up and rank them—who is important, who isn't important, who is desirable, who is less desirable—at some point in time, sooner or later, we have to recognize that we all are human. And we're all a whole lot more like each other than sometimes we like to think.

As I said to you, one thing will trigger another story for us that's sometimes not connected and at other times it is very deeply connected. So, to paraphrase Exodus 12:22, God says to the Hebrew people, "You're going to sacrifice a lamb and contain its blood in a bowl, and take a hyssop plant [a hyssop plant is like a flower that has a sponge on top of it], and you're going to use the hyssop plant like a sponge and you're going to put it into the blood and you're going to make a mark on the headboard above the door and on both sides of the door frame."

Hang in with me for one moment here. You're going to take the hyssop and dip it into the blood and make a mark on the headboard right where the crown of thorns would have been on Jesus's head and make a mark on both sides of the doorframe, right where his hands would have been nailed to the cross.

I can't hear this story and not remember the tremendous cost of God's love for me. I can't hear this story and not remember what God's love for me cost God.

REFLECTIONS BY RUTH A. DAUGHERTY

Every time I see the logo of the Reconciling Ministries Network displayed on a church or as part of its communications, I know it is a place where persons of differing sexual orientation and gender identity are welcome and are safe to participate fully in the life of the community. The rainbow colors remind me of the covenant that God made with "every living creature" (Genesis 9:16), that the world would be safe from destruction. The cross signifies the love and sacrifice of Jesus Christ for all humankind. For a church to be able to post this rainbow sign of reconciliation and acceptance requires much preparation.

At Grandview UMC, this preparation spanned over a decade. The sermons of the pastors frequently emphasized God's love for all persons and the reality that we often express that love verbally but fail to live it out in our actions toward LGBTQIA+ persons. Beth Stroud, lesbian ordained UMC clergy, was invited to speak about her experience of rejection and church trial at a Lenten luncheon. On another occasion, Rev. William Cherry, a UMC retired pastor, and Mark Stoner, a gay man, spoke in a Sunday morning worship service about their experiences of dialoguing and working together on their church's Sacred Worth Team for full inclusion of LGBTQIA+.[1] One Lenten season, the membership was challenged to read *The Year Of Living Biblically* and then attend a session with the author, A. J. Jacobs, who had attempted for a year to follow the requirements of the Israelites in the Hebrew Scriptures. This led to some lively discussion about the Scriptures we insist upon observing as written while ignoring other passages. This then led to questions about what God really requires of us in our practices and actions as well as beliefs.

The Searchers/Contemporary Issues Class continued to study and discuss what the Bible says and how to apply its teachings to our personal lives and our relationships especially with LGBTQIA+ persons. In 2013 the class initiated a call for Grandview to become a Reconciling Congregation. Contact was made with the UMC Reconciling Ministries Network for information about the process for officially becoming a Welcoming Congregation. We looked forward to being able to post the rainbow sign communicating publicly that Grandview is a safe, inclusive place for all people.

---

1. William Cherry is a former pastor of Grandview, serving this congregation from 1973–78.

Marge Cumpston: I am the mother of four daughters. My oldest is gay, my second is straight, my third is gay, and my fourth is straight, which is very unusual in family arrangements. They're usually bunched together. I have been working with this situation since I've known about my oldest daughter—for thirty-six years now and my younger one for thirty years. They are ten years apart in age. We didn't have any real coming-out story. It just sort of evolved. There were not a lot of boys around the house. There were certainly plenty of girls and very interesting music: Holly Near and Meg Christian—"You know what? I think this kid is gay. Well, I'll be dog-gone. Isn't that interesting?" And that was the way it went.

I was working at a boy's school and was hearing a lot of words I didn't like, not knowing how to handle it. And I went to an organization named PFLAG[2] and learned to say, "Someone I know and love very much is gay and you've just hurt my feelings," when I heard the words I didn't want to hear. So that was my learning process. And in the course of going to PFLAG, I heard some of the funniest coming-out stories. They were hysterical!

I went to my oldest, and I said, "Why didn't we have a coming-out story? I don't have any coming-out story here." We were in a Unitarian Church at the time, and she said, "Mom, neither my home nor my church ever told me anything was wrong." And I thought, that's what Grandview has become. You have no idea what you've done for young people, very young people, by allowing them to be who they are and never telling them there's anything wrong with them.

TESTIMONY BY MARY MERRIMAN

In my late teens, I left home to enter the military. I had wanted to go into the Army, but my dad said, "No, I don't want you to do that." His objection to the Army was that he didn't want me to meet "those people." I didn't understand what he was talking about. As the eldest daughter of an Irish Catholic family of twelve, my expectation was that I would someday marry a man and have children. No other views of human sexuality were considered or discussed.

So I went into the Air Force and knew nothing about homosexuality until a woman in my unit approached me and said, "I need to stay away from you, you know, I'm really attracted to you." And I remember telling

2. Formerly, "Parents, Families, and Friends of Lesbians and Gays." PFLAG, https://www.pflag.org.

Linda, you know, if my body could have reacted to my emotions, I would have been thrown back through so many walls. It was just such a shock. I eventually came out in the military, at least with other gay people, and it was always behind closed doors.

Life involved a lot of suspicion, uncertainty, and fear. Many friends died of suicide or succumbed to alcohol and/or drug addiction. The pressure to conform to a "straight lifestyle" was overwhelming given the fear of losing career, family, and friends for not doing so.

Coming out wasn't easy or linear. I didn't wake up one day and say, "I'm gay." In my "questioning" period, I did what was expected and supported and had a boyfriend. And it wasn't that I didn't love him. I did, in my own way. We were together for several months, and I became pregnant. Before either of us knew I was pregnant, he met someone else, and they married. I left the military when it was learned that I was pregnant.

In 1969 at nineteen years old, pregnant and with one foot in the closet and one foot out, I had to make some decisions about my son's care. With no role models that I knew of, the gay community wanted me to raise this child. But it wasn't a good environment for raising kids as a single parent. At that time, "out of wedlock" and "bastard" were words used on birth certificates, and I didn't want my son labeled in that way. My family wanted to help, but there were eight other children in a small apartment. I came to the belief that single parenting as a lesbian in 1970 was not a healthy way to raise a baby, and the only reasonable decision I had was to find a family to raise my son. I was blessed in finding a family who loved and cared for him. So we agreed to an adoption.

I kept the secret of my sexual orientation from my family until a few years after I was discharged from the service. I was in college and it was 1974. Homosexuality had been officially removed from the list of mental illnesses and college campuses were forming gay clubs. I had met my first serious relationship and called to tell my parents the good news. My biological family was large and close with one another and seemed to be very accepting of differences among people. I was taken back when the reaction I got was not welcoming and affirming. By 1976, my parents and I severed our ties with one another, and with that, my relationship with my nine brothers and sisters was ended as well . . . for a time. My family and I didn't communicate until 1986 when my sister called to say that my parents wanted to meet with me while they were visiting my mom's brother and sister-in-law in St. Petersburg, Florida.

The meeting was strained, especially given my apprehension with my mom's sister-in-law, who professed herself as an evangelical Christian. I anxiously expected that at some point she would hurl one of the clobber verses about homosexuality and I would be expected to defend my sexual orientation again. Instead, my aunt was warm and courteous. After hearing about my role as a pastor, she donated my uncle's electronic organ to my church! Together, we talked in general terms about my work at Good News MCC but little about the conflicts that had separated my parents and me for ten years. At the end of our visit, my dad and mom met with me privately in my aunt's driveway to apologize for the separation and to assure me that they didn't really believe I could be doing anything "that wrong" as to break up our family. I took that to mean that they no longer regarded my sexual orientation as so evil that it should separate us from one another. It was their way of opening further dialogue with me. They returned home to Blue Island, Illinois, where I grew up. Jan and I visited once and got to know my parents and my nine siblings.

A few months after our initial visit, mom called to say that dad was ill. Dad was diagnosed with colon cancer and died in September of 1986. I regret not having more time with my dad to continue to resolve our concerns with one another and to rebuild our once strong relationship. My relationship with mom continued until her death in 2001, and the relationship with my siblings continues to be strong and affirming.

The coming-out process is very complicated. It's not only saying, "I'm gay," but also dealing with all the moments in life and how much healing has to take place. And it's the reason that I stay at Grandview. I don't like the United Methodist statement of exclusion, but the reason that I stay is that grace overwhelms wrong. When I first got to Grandview, I was really questioning a lot about faith, very uncertain of the direction my faith was going to take. When I finally started making more commitments at Grandview, I met with Pastor Andrea to say that it was really going to require a lot of healing to bring me to a place where I could begin to articulate life in the context of faith in God again. I think God continues to work through us, and I think those are our coming-out stories. So there's been a lot of coming out story going on for me here at Grandview. I am amazed at how my faith has grown. I'm in awe of how God has worked through so many different challenges in my life.

8

Committing to the Journey
Exodus 12:37—15:21

"THE JOURNEY OUT" BY ANDREA BROWN

One of the things that really strikes me when I hear this story is that God knows us well. All of us.

God knows us Israelites, we who have been knocked down, over and over again, for a long, long time by whatever chains hold us: chains of debt and discouragement and doubt; chains of a work-life that threatens to swallow us whole; chains of self-pity or self-hatred or self-centeredness; chains of tasks left undone, every "sorry" left unsaid; chains of prejudice and abuses of power that limit our ability to be known and treated as equals. Yes, God knows us Israelites. God knows that we don't have a whole lot of fight in us. We do not relish conflict, and we're fickle: we hate being enslaved; we want to be freed; we hate freedom; we want to go back.

So God leads us out by a roundabout route—away from an immediate clash with an as-yet-unknown hostile army (call them the Philistines if you want) so that we don't become discouraged or wearied right away by more fighting. God knows we Israelites need time to recover. So freedom doesn't come as directly as we wish it would, but it comes, apparently, the only way it can.

God knows us Egyptians, too—we who have enjoyed our privileged position for a long, long time. God knows that even ten plagues, even death itself, will not convince us. We're nothing if not hard-hearted, and we're fickle too: we'll shove the Israelites out the door, but then we'll chase after them. After all, who will do our heavy lifting for us? Freedom, God knows, is never, finally, *given* by us oppressors. It must always be *won* by the oppressed.

God also knows us leaders, the Moseses who will forget the gifts God has already given us. "Why do you cry out to *me*?" God asks. "*You* do it, Moses," God says to us. "Lift up your staff, and stretch out your hand over the sea and divide it" (Exodus 14:16). God knows we will think this is crazy, but lacking something better to do, we just might try it.

I once heard a pilot asked what he would do if he was flying a 747 with almost 500 souls aboard and the plane started having engine trouble. He was a religious man, and the person asking the question expected him to say he'd pray. But he said he wouldn't pray. Instead, he said, he'd focus all his energies on righting that plane. That seems to be what God is asking Moses to do: don't ask me for help right now; use the gifts with which I've already equipped you. Bring all that you have—physically, emotionally, and spiritually—bring all of it to bear. *You* can save people if only you will.

But of course, a person alone *cannot* divide a sea. It seems clear that people *alone* cannot fix the Middle East. How many times do we have to prove that to ourselves? People *alone* cannot overcome racism in the United States. People *alone* cannot figure out how to cure mental illnesses so that we do not have to lose another Robin Williams, another beloved grandchild, or any other tormented soul. There are times when we just can't figure it out—or we *can* figure out what's wrong, but we still can't solve it. We are stuck between the army and the sea. In such situations, this story suggests, we need only do one thing: stay with the one God sent. Stay with Moses. Stay with Jesus. And the way will open up to us.

The Israelites are on the shore when they see Pharaoh's terrifying army approaching with all its war machines—its chariots and spears and armor almost as fearsome a sight as police in gas masks and Plexiglas shields with armored vehicles, helicopters, and semi-automatic weapons. It is as fearsome as the advancing army of depression, disease, and the specter of aging or joblessness. There's nowhere left for the Israelites to turn, and Moses has the audacity to say to them, "Do not be afraid, stand firm, and see the deliverance that the Lord will accomplish for you today" (Exodus 14:13).

"The Lord will fight for you. You have only to keep still." It reminds me of what President Abraham Lincoln told himself: "Be sure to put your feet in the right place, then stand firm." Plant your feet in the right place, stand firm, and God will accomplish for you.

The Sea of Reeds parts. God makes a way when there *is no way*—when there is no place left to turn. God knows it will not happen overnight; but God also knows that all Egyptian armies are made of sand. They may look fierce when they are coming at you in chariots and armor, dressed in riot gear or expensive suits. But when it comes right down to it, they are made of sand. Eventually, a wave will rise up, and they will be no more. Mourning and crying and pain will be no more.

As our last act of worship today, we're going to make offerings to the God who is a way-maker as we listen to, and move with, this sea-parting God. You could even say this God is "The Boss"—in the best sense of the word. We'll play Bruce Springsteen's version of "O Mary, Don't You Weep."[1]

What a testament to faith in the unseen and the unrealized when we recall that this song was written by enslaved people in America for enslaved people in America. It's a song addressed to a grieving mother, Mary, on the day after Good Friday, when Easter was not yet known. It's a song for a mother mourning a son dying of Ebola in Sierra Leone or a daughter dying of starvation in the hills of Iraq, surrounded by a hostile army with no apparent path out. This is a song sung to a father living in Gaza cradling his war-wounded child, a song for the children of Holocaust survivors, who simply want a safe place to call home. It's a song for children who are taking a dangerous train ride north today to escape the "army" that threatens to conscript them into gangs or force them to work as child prostitutes. It's a song for people caught up in, and weighed down by, chains of worry and conflict and fear and addiction, of loneliness and grief, and systems that aren't working the way they are supposed to.

It's the promise that God will come through—a plea to trust that evil will not have the last word. Sometimes, all we can do is sing it; cling to it. Or let others sing it for us when we don't have enough hope in our lungs to sing it for ourselves. It's a song for you and me, so I invite you to come forward on the dry ground of the middle aisle, bring your gifts to God, and sing along with the chorus. Weep, if you must, and let your friends catch your tears. Dance, if you can, and give thanks for a time when God made a

1. Springsteen, "O Mary Don't You Weep."

way for you. Pass that gift on to others. Sing, that the way may be open to all God's people one day—one day, soon.

REFLECTIONS BY RUTH A. DAUGHERTY

One of the often-spoken sayings by my mother was: "Actions speak louder than words!" She added, it is easy to say what we believe, but it only becomes a reality through our actions both for ourselves and for others to witness. Thus, after verbally affirming the understanding of God's inclusive love for all people including LGBTQIA+ persons, I made the commitment to read and study Scripture more intensely; to join with groups that advocated inclusiveness; to have conversations with persons of different views; to encourage dialogue in the Searchers class; to speak for change in exclusionary language in the United Methodist *Discipline*; and to work with the pastors and other church members to become a Reconciling Congregation.

In 2013 the Searchers/Contemporary Issues Class initiated a call for Grandview to become a Reconciling Congregation. Contact was made with the United Methodist Reconciling Ministries Network for information about becoming a Reconciling Congregation. The pastors asked me to be a member of the team to develop the agenda for becoming a Reconciling Congregation and to draft a statement to be presented to the Church Council.

In January, 2014, the congregation was invited to attend special sessions sponsored by the Searchers/Contemporary Issues Class. These included: 1) Bible study by the Rev. William Cherry, a retired United Methodist pastor; 2) experiences as a lesbian and a pastor in Metropolitan Community Church by the Rev. Mary Merriman; 3) experiences as parents of gay and lesbian children by three couples from Grandview UMC; 4) the polity of The United Methodist Church as it relates to attempts to change the *Book of Discipline*'s policies on same-sex marriage and ordination of "self-avowed practicing homosexuals" and discussion of becoming a Reconciling Congregation.

In February, 2014, the Church Council was asked to endorse the Welcoming Statement developed by the team appointed by the pastors to become a Reconciling Congregation (see Introduction). A question was raised about why this written statement had to be adopted when our web site already has a statement indicating we are welcoming. To become a Reconciling Congregation, a statement must include specific reference to sexual orientation and gender identity because specific words can indicate those persons who are presently being excluded from full participation. After extensive discussion, the Council unanimously adopted the statement.

The Council also adopted a process leading to the congregation's voting on becoming a Reconciling Congregation.

Sunday, February 16—Information table in the Gathering Space and announcement of a survey the following week.

Sunday, February 23—Survey in worship services including three questions about the Welcoming Statement:

1. If the vote were held today would you support Grandview Church adopting the [welcoming] statement?

2. What questions would you like to have addressed?

3. If you would like one of the pastors or a member of the Reconciling Team to respond to you personally, please include your name and an email address or phone number.

Monday, February 24—Reconciling Team meets to review the results of the survey, to respond to questions, and to plan next steps.

Sunday, March 2—Announce survey results, include responses in bulletin, give explanatory information, and invite persons for conversations hosted by the Reconciling Team at noon, following worship.

Wednesday, March 12—Church Council finalizes any decisions. It was agreed that the desired percentage of votes to approve becoming Reconciling Congregation would be 75 percent. Process of voting was established to assure anonymity of the voter and one person, one vote.

Sundays, March 16 and 23—Congregational vote was taken.

Sunday, March 30—Results of the vote was announced (93 percent voted yes) and the statement was posted.

The words of the adopted statement clearly indicate the belief of Grandview that all persons are welcomed to participate fully in our community of faith. Grandview is committed to implement those words with actions.

Connie Brown: My husband Alan was assigned as an assistant pastor at a large congregation in Pennsylvania. Various people just came to him because he gradually became known as a good listener and counselor. He was finding he was getting stories of persons and families who were saying, "I've got this problem, I can't tell anybody about it, but I can tell you, pastor." I didn't know many of the stories, but occasionally, as the spouse of a pastor, I would be the listening ear for my husband, and it wouldn't go farther than that. You could see there certainly were needs out there. For example, there was this wonderful family who had a son who had lived in New York City, active with a well-known musical group and came back here to die, of AIDS. There was a fine man in the congregation married to a woman, who came to talk. She said, "We are getting a divorce, and that is because my husband has determined that he is gay. But I want him to be treated with regard and respect. I am not rejecting him." So, that opened things for the pastors to indeed be nurturing.

Gardette (Lou) Cumpston is a retired communication engineer living in a retirement community in Lancaster. He is the father of four children, two boys and two girls. One of the girls is gay. He is married to Marge and is the stepfather to four girls, two of which are gay. Lou is a member of Grandview UMC and active in several gay rights organizations.

Marge and I came to this area about three and a half years ago when we moved into a retirement community. We have breakfast as a group, and that's the only time we get together as a group and eat. Marge and I have been rather open, not hiding the fact that she has two daughters who are lesbians. I have one. We've been quite open about that; we've had the girls go to breakfast any number of times.

About a year ago, we were interviewed for an article in the newspaper about our work with PFLAG, getting a PFLAG chapter started again. So they took a picture, and it was a very nice article. And we kind of wondered, well, what's going to happen now? We ended up getting about 8–10 copies of the article stuck under our door, "Thought you might like another copy," this sort of thing. There was a much different attitude than I thought we might get from a group of old folks like us, and I thought that was rather interesting. Also, they were aware and tracking with us what was happening with Frank Schaefer and his trial.

The people most interested were a Catholic couple with a lesbian daughter. I'd have to say, they were rather envious of how open things were and how what has happened with Frank over a period of time has not been all that bad for him. I think they're rather pleased. There's an attitude change going on. A lot of comment was, "Gosh, that's quite a church you belong to!"

Andrea Brown: The action of becoming open and affirming meant a lot to my family. Before we became a Reconciling Congregation, my kids were not out. I don't know how much that actual stance on the part of the church played into their coming out, but I think it made a difference. I think there's something about not secret keeping—which churches tend to be good at—that affects people's ability to be who they are, whether it's around issues of gender or sexuality or other issues, too. I think there's something about becoming open and affirming that is really healthy for a church in terms of breaking down secrets that make people hide the pieces of themselves that could be open. So, I'm really grateful for that.

The weekend of my ordination was the weekend that my niece Kate, who is transgender, really came out for the first time, was dressed in public as female for the first time ever. The ordination ceremony at annual conference is after a long day of meetings, and in the very last hour of those meetings, people were saying horrible, horrible things—the kind of conversation that we have annually at annual conference about gay and lesbian people, using the Bible in ways that the Bible is not meant to be used, as a cudgel instead of a love letter. And I kept praying that she and my brother and sister-in-law and my kids would not get there early and have to hear that. Fortunately, they did not.

For Kate, coming here to Grandview on Sunday morning for my celebration was such a positive experience of church. I don't remember exactly what Tim Riggs's message was that day, but there was something particularly warm and open, and she found herself in a metaphorical embrace. Kate's family had been a part of a Reconciling Congregation in California, but they hadn't been part of a church for a while since. So, for them as a family to have that positive experience meant the world to me.

TESTIMONY BY MARY MERRIMAN

Lancaster, Pennsylvania, has a long history as a peace and justice community. In the 1960s, the city and county created a local commission to seek remedies to discrimination in housing, education, employment, and public accommodations. The commission was also unique as it was a joint commission, requiring a cooperative relationship between the City Council and County Commissioners to maintain stability. For about twenty-five years, enforcement was up to the state Human Relations Commission. As the county is not able to make and enforce laws, the commission could only investigate. It needed the authority of a municipality, the Lancaster

City Council, to enforce its findings concerning complaints of discrimination against protected classes. In the spring of 1990, the Joint City-County Human Relations Commission sought enforcement powers.

I received a phone call from Linda Martin, then President of the Lancaster Chapter of the National Organization of Women. She had been invited to bring testimony to the Lancaster City Council about discrimination. Linda asked me to speak to the needs of lesbian and gay people in Lancaster, and she would address the needs of single moms with children. Linda spoke first, and then I gave my testimony. Stunned, I listened as Ingrid Ruoff and Charlie Bonner advanced a motion to amend the Lancaster County Human Relations Ordinance to add lesbian and gay people and familial status to the list of protected classes. Gender expression and identity were also added to the proposed legislation.

Adding protected classes—especially sexual orientation and gender expression/identity—was not a winning proposition in many areas of Lancaster County, sometimes referred to as the belt buckle of the Bible belt. The Lancaster County Commissioners would not support the addition of LGBT and familial status as protected classes and threatened to sever the unique relationship with the City Council if it adopted the proposed legislation. During one work session, a member of the City-County Human Relations Commission challenged that we had no right to seek an addition to the human relations ordinance as we had not shed enough blood yet.

Ironically, violence toward LGBT persons on Lancaster streets was on the increase. People were beaten who were "perceived" to be gay. We formed a night watch to escort LGBT persons into the Tally Ho gay bar because LGBT persons were being knifed and beaten. Religious zealots came to council meetings with Bibles in hand ranting of God's rejection of sexual orientation. Letters to the editor against LGBT people appeared daily for the three months before the legislation was voted upon. The Ku Klux Klan marched, taking advantage of the chaos within Lancaster County. Nancy Helms, a member of the Pink Triangle Coalition, opened a gay bookstore known as "The Closet" on Prince Street. The Closet was bombed twice and closed within its first year of operation.

When the local bookstore was bombed, the host congregation for Vision of Hope MCC—the Lancaster Metaphysical Chapel—became concerned that their facility might also be bombed. Vision of Hope was asked to leave the facility immediately after the publication of a newspaper article about the appearance of Rita Adessa—the executive director of the

Philadelphia Lesbian and Gay Task Force. We searched churches through-out the region but found none that would extend an invitation to hold our worship services in their facility. Barriers included fear, I'm sure, but more often were the prohibitive, financial costs. We then approached the Friends Meeting House, which agreed to lease space for our worship services for two years. We welcomed having a place to worship and the opportunity to continue to build our congregation.

Not much seemed to occur over the next two years. We continued to work on an amendment to the Human Relations Ordinance to include LGBT. We also worked for passage of a hate-crimes amendment with the help of Pink Triangle Coalition, Vision of Hope MCC, the men's and wom-en's potlucks, PFLAG, the Gay and Lesbian Helpline, the YWCA, Friends, and the Unitarians. Our base of support continued to evolve and included organizations like Shaarai Shomayim, Leadership Lancaster, Allies of Franklin and Marshall College, Elizabethtown College, and Millersville University. At various times, I would be told by people from the commu-nity to let them know if ever Vision of Hope MCC decided to purchase a facility. Unfortunately, I never recorded specific names.

The two years passed, and Friends was also growing and needed to use more of their facility. Hence, we did not renew our lease. I looked again for facilities to rent, but the cost of commercial space was very high and would not lead to ownership and control of our own property and program. The District Coordinator for the Mid-Atlantic District of the Universal Fellow-ship of Metropolitan Community Churches was residing in Lancaster and spotted a for-sale sign on a church property in Mountville, Pennsylvania. The property was owned by Trinity Reformed United Church of Christ. (Trinity was not an affirming congregation at that time but has since be-come one.) After contacting the church about the price of the sale and investigating ways for financing a purchase, I approached Vision of Hope MCC members. We had forty members at the time and the asking price was $165,000. We had no down payment, building fund, or any resources to make the purchase at the time. We were still traumatized by the conflict that we had experienced two years prior when we moved to Friends.

Admittedly, I was cautious, and our members were afraid. However, we've always seen God's hand in our journey. In 1973, homosexuality was removed from the list of mental illness disorders by the American Psychi-atric Association. HIV/AIDS was decimating our communities, but it was now being addressed by the national government, and medications were emerging that allowed us to live with HIV/AIDS. In the 1980s, private, consensual, same-sex activity was decriminalized in many, though not in all, states.[2] A city human-relations ordinance existed in Lancaster, and it seemed promising that a state ordinance would pass fairly soon. We were enjoying a period of peace as the level of assaults had died down along with the rhetoric. While afraid, we had reason for confidence that we should take the next step and investigate the possibility of a purchase. Numerous churches were having success with passing a bond for building purchases.

I contacted a frequently used bond company and learned that we would first need $20,000 to initiate the bond process. I approached a friend of the congregation who indicated he would loan the $20,000 without interest, to be repaid within six months. I brought the offer to the congregation and members of the church formed a fundraising plan and developed a schedule of activities by which we would work to return the $20,000 investment. The congregation saw these as signs that God favored our decisions and agreed to funding a bond issue for $165,000 (which included the $20,000 loan repayment plan). I didn't have a list of donors but did schedule meetings with all of the organizations and members and friends of Vision of Hope MCC to seek the needed funds and to identify bond purchasers. I then put together a press release announcing the purchase of the property.

The press release appeared in the Lancaster Intelligencer. It was either that morning or shortly thereafter that I received a phone call from a state police trooper, Joe, who asked for the date when we expected to enter the Mountville church property. I explained that we didn't have an absolute date but gave him a projected date of August 1993—approximately six months hence. Joe then informed me that the federal, state, and local law enforcement agencies would be working together to assure our safe passage into the building. We hung up, and I prayed, shaken and wondering how the change had occurred from 1991 when we had so much violence and chaos in Lancaster. We had fair support from law enforcement in 1991, but Joe's call indicated a kind of proactive engagement in 1993 that I had thought not possible and hoped would not be necessary.

No sooner had the newspaper announcement appeared than chaos seemed to start to break out in the newspapers and in Mountville. The Mountville borough began an active campaign, it seemed, requesting every

2. It took nearly two decades for same-sex activity to be decriminalized across the country. A 2003 U.S. Supreme Court decision, *Lawrence v. Texas*, made consensual, same-sex sexual activity legal, overturning its 1986 decision, *Bowers v. Hardwick*, which upheld an anti-sodomy statute in Georgia.

legal document that we had in order to demonstrate that we were a bona fide religious organization. My spouse Ruth was our realtor and went to the Mountville borough office every day with yet another document as requested by the borough council. Meanwhile, flyers started appearing in doors around Mountville protesting our purchase of the church property. The groups that the fliers represented were citizens of Mountville who opposed gay and lesbian people and often labeled us as sinners and perverts. The perversions cited included child molestation, bestiality, and sex orgies on the altar. Letters to the editor from people all over Lancaster denounced homosexuality as offensive before God. Media from Lancaster, Harrisburg, and around the United States told of the conflict with the Mountville community—but not without elements of sensationalism. In addition, thirty clergy from Lancaster County churches wrote a letter opposing our purchase and submitted it to the newspaper. A drawing appeared in a Harrisburg editorial picturing a community throwing rocks at Vision of Hope.

This would seem like more of the same as we had experienced in 1991, but an essential difference began to emerge. The Lancaster County Council of Churches voted to recognize Vision of Hope MCC's right to worship. Their resolution of May 17, 1993, entitled "Freedom of Religion in Lancaster County," called on "all civil and religious leaders to respect the right of Vision of Hope MCC to gather for worship without harassment or fear of molestation and to convey to their respective constituencies the need for such respect." Letters to the editor that were supportive and positive were written. In the previous conflict, there were few letters of support or protest against those who were against us in Lancaster County. My understanding of that time was that progressive people didn't feel that speaking out was useful and that we would be okay. Two years later, the lesson was learned and support became more apparent.

Allies—whether churches, organizations or individuals—attested to positive relationships with Vision of Hope. Most importantly, support emerged from one local Mountville church that was crucial to our success in purchasing our church home. Dean, then pastor of Mountville Church of the Brethren, called me to indicate that, sadly, he knew some of the people writing letters to the editor against our purchasing the property. Dean felt that he and his associate pastor might be able to facilitate better communication between Vision of Hope MCC and the writers. He would extend an invitation to those whom he knew and perhaps some other residents of Mountville who were opposed to our move to Mountville if we would do the same, inviting members of Vision of Hope MCC to join the discussion circles with the Mountville residents. We agreed that the discussions would not be made known to the press.

Both Dean and I were able to get participants for the conversation groups. In these groups, we shared stories of ourselves and our families, the type of employment (if any) we had, and our concerns regarding Vision of Hope's move to Mountville. The discussions were frank but respectful and challenged all of our assumptions about one another. Over time we learned that the concerns were genuine and not frivolous. We also learned that the concerns were sometimes formed by misconceptions and misunderstandings about one another's cultures. For instance, the notion that lesbian, gay, bisexual, and transgender people are pedophiles is sometimes due to stereotypes. However, sometimes it's also due to the pain that is experienced by too many children who are being sexually molested today. A large percentage of the time, children are molested by heterosexuals but sometimes by homosexuals. Another misconception is that homosexuality is selective and not preconditioned. Evidence continues to mount that homosexuality is preconditioned and not a choice. All of these myths and truths were discussed and the outcome was truly amazing.

One evening, I was presenting yet another speech about Vision of Hope MCC to the borough council, further answering questions about our church and non-profit status and once more stating that we intended to complete the purchase of the property. The room was packed. There was no escape through the front entrance of the Borough Hall. Concerned for my safety, some of my friends had arranged for a "get-away car" out of the borough office following my speech. I left the room but knew that people were there in the borough chambers recording every word and the name of every person speaking as another step in keeping Vision of Hope safe.

The press was present to record an amazing presentation from one of the women who had led the protest against our purchase of the church property. She told of our conversations at Mountville Church of the Brethren, as she was a part of all of them. She told of what she had learned of herself, her community, and of Vision of Hope MCC. She then withdrew her opposition to our purchase of the property. She and her husband became our next-door neighbors and friends for some time to follow.

In the month following the purchase, Dean tried to take one more step in assisting Vision of Hope MCC to become part of the worship community of Mountville. He talked with the Mountville Ministerium, and I was invited to join the next lunch meeting to talk about Vision of Hope MCC and our ministry. While I was anxious, I thought the discussion was a productive beginning. A week later I received a call from Dean. He was contrite in stating that the Mountville Ministerium had voted against Vision of Hope MCC joining.

Our move into the facility was not without apprehension. One hundred seventy-five people attended our opening worship, including new friends from Mountville, clergy from local churches, elected officials, and people of the LGBT community. Brinks Security was guarding me throughout the worship—and without my consent (others had set up the detail). A picture was taken of the sanctuary. Only one person was sitting in the congregation. When the person who wrote the article tried to get others to appear on camera in a picture being printed in the paper, many refused. The truth was that many people were closeted at the time. The movement to "out" people and to come out was only just beginning to find political traction. So it was different then than it is now. A lot has changed.

We completed the bond issue in March of 1994. It was a snowy day when we held our final rally to finish the sale. We had raised the $20,000 to return to our benefactor, and we eventually completed funding the $165,000 bond issue. I served as the pastor of Vision of Hope Metropolitan Community Church from 1987 to 1995.

ACT IV

Figuring Out in a New Voice

"We believe the church needs to pray for a sensitivity to be aware of and to respond to manifestations of the Holy Spirit in our world today. We are mindful that the problems of discerning between the true and fraudulent are considerable, but we must not allow the problems to paralyze our awareness of the Spirit's presence; nor should we permit our fear of the unknown and the unfamiliar to close our minds against being surprised by grace."

—The United Methodist General Conference[1]

"My nephew Alex was christened today at Grandview United Methodist Church in Lancaster, PA. It was the single most inclusive religious service I've ever been to, and they covered A LOT of material that you wouldn't expect to hear at church: income inequality, gender identity, gender discrimination, sexual orientation, and racism with an incredibly touching tribute to those who lost their lives in Charleston this week. The messages they told celebrated difference, diversity, love, and community. I'm not a religious man by any stretch, but I walked away with a little bit of a smile on my face, happy to know that there are places where faith, personal growth, and personal difference can mutually exist for the sole purpose of living a better life and building strong communities. Dare I say, I was inspired—at Grandview United Methodist Church."

—Dr. William (Bill) McNavage, partnered gay man, upon visiting Grandview, testifying to his friends via Facebook

1. UMC, "Guidelines: The UMC and the Charismatic Movement," 685.

95

How do we figure out what to believe when the world is changing so quickly? What do we proclaim when we no longer believe what we were taught growing up? Finding a new voice amid profound social change, particularly in our understanding of sexuality and gender, is a difficult and vitally important task. Many congregations and entire denominations are in the process of figuring out how to express a new voice of faith. I suggest that we are experiencing nothing less than a holy disruption caused by the Spirit among us.

Theologically, United Methodists "affirm that sexuality is God's good gift to all persons."[2] The United Methodist Church has taught this affirmation for as long as it has denounced homosexuality. I remember attending a training workshop on our Social Principles as a college student and being astounded to learn that my church taught such a positive view of sex. Surely, our bodies are important to the life of faith. However, Christians have expressed discomfort with and downright hostility toward sexuality since the time of Paul. This hostility to our embodied nature is most destructive when the tension between God's good creation and our human proclivity to sin is resolved through a patriarchal lens. Patriarchal structures, typically reinforced by misogynistic beliefs and behaviors, make it nearly impossible to live fully into our affirmation of the goodness of sexuality.

What shall we do as faithful Christians figuring it out—or as Paul encourages, working out our own salvation with fear and trembling (Philippians 2:12)? How can we remain faithful to God while open to the strange (perhaps even queer) experiences of our brothers and sisters in Christ?

The United Methodist Church "plead[s] for a spirit of openness and love" when maintaining community and ministry with persons who have diverse understandings and experiences with the Holy Spirit.[3] This church offers the following advice: "We commend to the attention of the church the affirmations of Paul on the importance of love in First Corinthians 13 and of Wesley—'In essentials, unity; in nonessentials, liberty; and, in all things, charity' (love that cares and understands). Without an active, calm, objective, and loving understanding of the religious experience of others, however different from one's own, harmony is impossible."

Theologically, this United Methodist statement is rooted in the idea of *charism*. According to the World Council of Churches, *charism* "denotes

---

2. UMC, *The Book of Discipline 2016*, para. 161.G.

3. UMC, "Guidelines: The UMC and the Charismatic Movement," 685. Subsequent unattributed quotes in this section are from the same document.

the gifts bestowed by the Holy Spirit on any member of the body of Christ for the building up of the community and fulfillment of its calling."[4] While embracing popular tools, such as spiritual gift inventories, in recent years, mainline Christian congregations are typically unaware of their own significant role in the assessment and affirmation of *charism*. The best example comes when a person declares to a local congregation that he or she senses a call to ministry, perhaps as a full-time religious vocation. It's then the congregation's responsibility to test and affirm the authenticity of such a perception.

The same is true of all spiritual gifts. "The criteria by which we understand another's religious experience must include its compatibility with the mind and the spirit of our Lord Jesus Christ, as revealed in the New Testament," explains the UMC. We recognize the Spirit by its fruit.

> If the consequence and quality of a reported encounter with the Holy Spirit leads to self-righteousness, hostility, and exaggerated claims of knowledge and power, then the experience is subject to serious question. However, when the experience clearly results in new dimensions of love, faith, joy, and blessings to others, we must conclude that this is "what the Lord hath done" and offer God our praise. "You will know them by their fruit" (Matthew 7:20).

I have witnessed this fruit in open and affirming congregations.

Open and affirming congregations exhibit the *charism* of radically inclusive love, expressed through ministries with persons of all sexual orientations and gender identities, whether single or married. Radically inclusive *agape* within open and affirming congregations serves as evidence of the Holy Spirit building up the church. The UMC's reaffirmation represents hope for Christians of all denominations who have experienced this gift. The UMC offers the following specific guidelines:

- Be open and accepting of those whose Christian experiences differ from your own.

- Continually undergird and envelop all discussions, conferences, meetings, and persons in prayer.

- Be open to new ways in which God by the Spirit may be speaking to the church.

---

4. World Council of Churches, *Baptism, Eucharist, and Ministry*, Ministry II.7a. This discussion is excerpted from Stephens, "In Landslide Vote."

- Avoid the temptation to force your personal views and experiences on others. Seek to understand those whose spiritual experiences differ from your own.

- [For pastors:] Pray for the gifts of the Spirit essential for your ministry; continually examine your life for the fruits of the Spirit.

- Do not be disturbed if your experience is not the same as others. The work and mission of a healthy congregation calls for many gifts (1 Corinthians 12–14). Each Christian is a unique member of the body of Christ and should seek to discover his or her gifts and role.

- Pray continuously for sensitivity to the will and the leading of the Holy Spirit.

Perhaps the Holy Spirit will give new voice to persons experiencing the gift of radically inclusive, open and affirming love in Christian community. Perhaps wrestling with our past and looking toward God's good future, we may begin to figure it out—if not all of it, at least enough to guide us through today even if we remain unsure about tomorrow.

In Act IV, the story of Exodus meets the resurrection of Christ. In chapter 9, "Second Thoughts," Michael Alleman offers a word of hope to folks in the wilderness of change in his sermon, "In the Wilderness and Longing to Go Back." Ruth Daugherty reflects on changes significant to her own life and the importance of preparation for change at Grandview.

Chapter 10, "Idols and Images," begins with my sermon "Turning Point," expressing the convictions underlying this entire book. In this sermon, I preach about the golden calf incident and the dangers of idolatry—even the possibility of "open and affirming ministry" becoming an idol. Ruth Daugherty reflects on disparate images of God she's experienced in her life and their theological importance. Connie Brown shares one reaction to a gay Sunday School teacher in a congregation she previously attended.

Chapter 11, "Easter Proclamation," includes stories of love and resurrection. Andrea Brown emphatically proclaims "Love Trumps All" following a contentious and acerbic church trial, offering an Easter message in a sermon originally preached in November. Ruth Daugherty meditates on the resurrection in a reflection titled, "Life in the Midst of Death." Mary Merriman closes Act IV, sharing testimony about her heart attack in 1994, subsequent retirement from MCC ministry, and return to ministry nearly twenty years later, at Grandview.

9

Second Thoughts
Exodus 15:22–27; 16:1–3, 11–15, 32–33; 17:1–7

"IN THE WILDERNESS AND LONGING TO GO BACK"
BY MICHAEL I. ALLEMAN

I remember hearing an old story of a farmer who was putting a tin roof on his barn. As he was putting this tin roof on, he slipped and began sliding down the roof of his barn. Immediately, he prayed, "Lord, help me!" And with that—before the words were even out of his mouth—his pants caught on a nail and he stopped sliding down. The farmer looked up to heaven and said, "That's okay God. I got this." I thought about this story when I reflected upon today's Scripture lesson.

Throughout this study of the Exodus story, we have read how God heard the cries of the Israelites to be freed from their slavery. We've read how God called Moses and Aaron to go to Pharaoh demanding he let their people go, but Pharaoh would have none of it. So God visited ten plagues upon Pharaoh and the Egyptians. At the last plague, when the angel of death visited upon every Egyptian home and had the first-born son in each home die, Pharaoh finally cried "uncle" and let the Israelites go. But the Israelites weren't even to the Sea of Reeds before Pharaoh changed his mind and started to gather up his army to go after them, to recapture them again. We've read how God separated the sea: the waters parted and wind came and dried up the land so that the Israelites walked through the sea on dry land. We've read the story of Pharaoh and his army following close behind, and as they got into the Reed Sea, the waters receded back again and washed over them and the army drowned, everyone including Pharaoh. So, here are the Israelites now, on the other side of the Sea of Reeds.

The Israelites have traveled three days and they're thirsty and the water is bitter. So, God tells Moses to throw this log into the water, which Moses does, and now the water is sweet and they can drink from it. Fast-forward two months and fifteen days: the people are still traveling in this desert; they are even more tired, thirsty, and hungry. They come to Moses and say, "What have you done? Brought us out here to die? We'd rather be back in slavery, at least there we knew where our food was coming from!" That's okay God, we've got this.

Did they not see God's hand at work in all of the events that had taken them to that place? Did they not believe that God was still working in their midst? It's not just this one time—if you continue to read through the Exodus story you'll find them griping time and time again. Finally, Moses says to them, "You realize, don't you, that you're not griping to me, you're griping to God."

Now, what I want to suggest to you is that maybe we're pretty much like the Israelites. And you might say, "Oh Mike, you're being pretty harsh on us here." Well then, let me rephrase it. Maybe the Israelites are pretty much like us. It's difficult when there's big change—huge changes—happening in our lives. It's difficult to get through them. When things change, when our world changes, it's hard to get through it.

Twenty-some years ago, Joel Barker used the phrase "paradigm shift" to name this reality.[1] Remember that? Barker said that everything changes, and it's so difficult and frustrating to know how to move forward. He used the example of watches, Swiss-made watches. At one point, the Swiss Watch Company controlled 80 percent of the world market for watches. They had it down; they knew how to do it. Not a better mainspring could be found than those of the Swiss watchmakers. Then, along came this thing called the electronic quartz watch. Within a decade, the worldwide watch market had shifted to Japan, with electronic quartz watches. Here's the ironic part: who is it that discovered the electronic quartz watch? An inventor at the Swiss Watch Company! Their own scientists developed an electronic quartz

1. Barker, "The New Business of Paradigms."

mechanism, but it didn't have a mainspring, so they thought, surely no one would be interested in it as a watch. They displayed it at a trade show where a couple of other companies noticed. These companies developed their own electronic prototypes and, within seven years, took 80 percent of the market share. The whole world changed for the Swiss.

What I'm suggesting to you is this: we would much rather continue doing the same thing, even when it becomes painful and difficult, than to try something new, something different. It's human nature. We'd much rather continue with the known than try something that we don't know—the unknown. An Arab chief shared this story of a Persian general who caught a spy and condemned him to death. Now this particular Persian general had a quirk in that everyone he put to death was given a choice: they could face the firing squad or they could face going through a large black door. So, when the spy came before the general and was sentenced to death, the general gave him the same choice: "Do you want the firing squad or this huge black door?" A difficult decision for him—it took a while. But eventually the spy finally said, "firing squad." And after the general heard the rifles firing, he turned to his aide and said, "They always choose the firing squad. They just can't handle the thought of the unknown." The aide turned to him and said, "Well what's behind the large, black door?" And the general replied, "Freedom—but very few have the courage to choose it."

Here's the rub. Ellen Glasgow said it well: "The only difference between a rut and a grave are the dimensions." What she's saying is that change is a part of life, to live is to change, to not change is to cease living. And that's true for the church. What's it mean for us to be followers of Jesus but for us to make disciples who transform the world? It might be different than it was yesterday. What's it mean for us to make disciples who transform the world *today?* That's always what we're called to be doing. I heard someone once say, "If you don't like change, you're going to like irrelevance even less."[2] Change comes because what we've got now is not working anymore. It's no longer working for us. We need to change, to find a different way of doing it.

Here at Grandview, I'm going to suggest for you that change is going to be a part of our future. I don't know what it means for us, but I do know that less than a year from now, I'm going to be gone, retired from pastoral ministry. Now we've been trying to put staff in place—excellent, gifted staff in place—so that that transition is going to be as smooth as possible, but it'll

2. Attributed to General Eric Shinseki, former chief of staff for the U.S. Army.

be different. I know there'll be some who say, "Yes! For twenty-one years I've been waiting to get rid of Mike and now finally he's gone!" And there will be others who say, "Well it's just not the same." Yeah, it won't be the same. My prayer is that it will be better. It'll be different, but it'll be better.

What I'm suggesting to you is that as the Israelites went into the wilderness, they were different people than they were when they came out. Look at the map that shows where the Israelites traveled in their forty years in the wilderness. You know, if you look at where they began and where they ended up, it's really a rather short distance. It wouldn't have taken long at all. But following their path, they travelled all around. Perhaps the reason it took forty years to get to their destination is because it took forty years for them to become the people they needed to be to enter into the land of milk and honey. The people who entered the Promised Land weren't the same people who entered into the wilderness. Those who came out were different. And we look at that and wonder, "How were they different, what changed?" They came out with the Ten Commandments. They came out with a communal leadership that would show them how to treat each other and those around them. They came out a different people than they were entering into the wilderness. They came out knowing that they were God's people.

So what's that mean for us here at Grandview? I don't know. I do know things are going to be different here—but even deeper than just here in Grandview Church. The United Methodist Church is changing. It's not working for us anymore so we have to find new ways of calling and making disciples to transform the world around us and find new ways that work for us in today's world. And it's not just The United Methodist Church—it's *all* churches in North America finding that it's not working. We have to find new ways to do it. And it's going to be difficult for us. And it's going to be challenging for us.

I remember when I was growing up, the mission field was very clear. I grew up in the Evangelical United Brethren Church, and for us, Sierra Leone was our mission field. We sent all of our missionaries and mission resources there. We knew where our mission field was: over there, on the other side of the ocean. Do you know where our mission field is today? It's right outside our doors. It's here, among the people we see everyday. Touching the lives around us in Grandview community. Touching the lives of the homeless children in the city of Lancaster, touching people in eastern Pennsylvania, and worldwide—touching the lives of other people.

But it begins right here in our own neighborhood. Christian mission has changed. The Church must change. This congregation must change.

"So how, then, are we like the Israelites, Mike?" Well this wilderness that we go through will have some pain to it, but I've lived through enough wildernesses to know the joy, the joy of hope that is offered in times of change, in difficult times.

When I'm talking about hope, hope is different from wishing. I know you've heard me say this before. Wishing is when you know exactly what you're wishing, for example, "I wish you a Merry Christmas." I know what I mean when I say that: "I want you to have great times with family, with friends, and feel their love and let them feel your love and to recognize Christ's presence with you always." That's what I mean when I say, "I wish you a Merry Christmas." Hope is not so clear.

Hope is what I hold onto when I don't know what the answer is. Hope is God making a way where we don't see a way. It's an active hope. I'm grateful to Gil Rendle, former Alban Institute consultant, who shared with us that St. Augustine used to talk about an active hope. He said this active hope had two daughters, Anger and Courage: Anger out of what could be and was not and Courage to make it happen. So maybe, maybe that's what we're going to be about. We're going to be talking with each other and the surrounding community about what it means to be living in God's kingdom, in God's ways, in God's realm. What's that look like? What's that taste like? What's that feel like? And after we've talked about it, we'll capture a glimpse of it and get angry at what could be and is not and then pray for God to give us the courage to make it happen. And in that way, maybe we will be a lot like the children of Israel. Maybe we will.

REFLECTIONS BY RUTH A. DAUGHERTY

Reflecting upon the changes that would be made at Grandview as a result of becoming a Reconciling Congregation, I recalled a "moving experience" of change I had when I was a pre-teen. Upon my father's return from the Virginia Annual Conference of the United Brethren Church, he announced that we were moving from Shenandoah, a city in Virginia, to Franklin, West Virginia, a small rural town. The move had to be made before the next Sunday, when he was to be in the pulpits of four of the seven churches on that charge.

I had mixed emotions about the move and the resulting changes. There was the excitement of going to a different geographic location and having new experiences, but it also meant leaving the familiar surroundings and routines. These emotions became conflicting realities following the move. There were adjustments, such as living in a house heated only by a wood stove in the living room and the wood burning range in the kitchen instead of heat supplied by a furnace in our former house. Being over forty miles from the nearest bakery meant bread delivery once a week during World War II, resulting in my learning to work with yeast dough to make bread for our family. At school, I felt like an outsider because my classmates had lived in the same area all of their lives.

At the same time, I had new adventures of hiking in the mountains, working with a friend harvesting hay, having teachers who were interested in me personally as well as academically, taking piano lessons in order to provide music for worship services, and becoming a member of the Otterbein Guild Girls Missionary Association.

As I look back at *all* of those experiences, I understand the ones I resented at that time as well as those I enjoyed made important contributions for the enrichment of my life and preparation for the future.

Grandview took time to prepare for the changes that would result from becoming a Reconciling Congregation. Some persons, while affirming the decision, had uncertainty about what might result. However, the changes that impacted the life and ministry of Grandview have been mostly positive. The rainbow sign of a Reconciling Congregation is posted on the outdoor bulletin board and in all church communications to announce publicly our affirmation of inclusiveness. At the time, Grandview was unique among the United Methodist churches in the Lancaster area as the only Reconciling Congregation. Members of the congregation have been freed to talk about their LGBTQIA+ children and relatives and to acknowledge their own sexual orientation and gender identity. Individuals and families have joined Grandview because they want to be part of an inclusive fellowship. The staff includes a retired ordained clergy of the Metropolitan Community Church as visitation pastor, Mary Merriman, and a lesbian musician who leads the Celebration Service.

This "moving experience" of Grandview UMC continues with sermons calling members to follow Christ's Way, groups studying the Bible while seeking guidance for daily living, volunteers using their talents and skills to respond to needs in the community and the world, and staff ministering in creative and compassionate ways.

10

Idols and Images
Exodus 32:1–14

"TURNING POINT" BY DARRYL W. STEPHENS

This is the story of two different faith communities, each experiencing a significant turning point in their journey with God. In the Exodus narrative, we read about a stiff-necked people following a once-reluctant leader called by a vaguely remembered deity of their distant ancestors. Who are these people? And who is this God of Israel?

The golden calf episode marks the defining moment for the Hebrews as they become the people of God. When the people build an idol, no one wants to claim them. Moses and God engage in mutual finger-pointing, much as two parents might argue about a disobedient child. Each of them saying, "*your* people . . ." (Exodus 32:7 and 11). This is a life-changing, identity-confirming, God-revealing, mercy-filled moment for the Hebrews. This is a turning point for the people Israel.

A turning point is a pivotal moment in the life of faith, in a relationship, or in the journey of a people. It is a dramatic scene in the drama of life. Theologically—that is, in relation to God—a turning point is *metanoia*, repentance. When we start off in one direction and slowly or suddenly realize that we are going the wrong way—and then make a course correction. Repentance is a change in heart and action, putting us back on track in our relationships with God and each other. At its most profound, repentance can mark a radical departure from our old ways; it can mark new birth and new identity. A turning point can also be a renewal of purpose rather than an about-face, a reaffirmation of one's core identity amidst new circumstances.

I think Grandview experienced such a turning point last year, when we voted to become a Reconciling Congregation. We, like the Israelites, must continually rediscover, remember, and remind ourselves of our common identity and mission. So, as we consider how the Israelites found themselves at this point in their journey, listen for what this text might mean for us today.

The story of Exodus is about new identities and newly recognized old identities. The book begins, "These are the names . . ." (Exodus 1:1) and proceeds to remind us of our ancestors in the faith, since perhaps we've forgotten just as the Hebrews have. When the enslaved Hebrews first cry out from bondage, they do not cry out to God—they just cry out! They do not know or remember God. And God, ever present and faithful, hears their unaddressed cry anyway. Then, God calls Moses to be their leader—a new identity for this sheepherder. Remember the burning bush?

Moses's calling is all about recognition and identity. When Moses realizes that this new role will require him to go before mighty Pharaoh and speak out on behalf of all the slaves, he balks and protests by questioning his and God's identity. His first protest is, "Who am I?" (Exodus 3:11). His second protest to Yahweh is, "Who are *you*?" You see, identity has a lot to do with recognition, being known by others for who you really are. Moses knew that the Hebrew slaves would not immediately recognize God or themselves as God's people. God at first answers enigmatically, "I AM WHO I AM" (Exodus 3:14). What kind of identification is that!?

As the story progresses, God establishes the identity of the Hebrews relationally. God is clear that the people will be known in relation to God, and that only then will they know who God is. God says, "I will take you as my people, and I will be your God. You shall know that I am the Lord your God, who has freed you from the burdens of the Egyptians" (Exodus 6:7). The Exodus story is about identity formation, as the Hebrews become known as (and know themselves to be) the people of God.

You remember the repeated refrain during the plague narratives. God says to Moses, go tell Pharaoh, "Let my people go!" These are God's people, according to God. Ten times prior to the golden calf incident, God claims this people as God's own.[1] While all of creation belongs to God, it is God's plan for Israel to be set apart, distinguished as God's people through a holy covenant. God promises to them, "You shall be for me a priestly kingdom and a holy nation" (Exodus 19:6). Five times during the plagues, God distinguishes the Hebrews from the Egyptians and offers them special protections.[2] The Passover, during which the Hebrews mark their doorframes with blood so that the angel of death will spare them, is the quintessential example of this.

Israel claims its identity as God's people by obeying God's commands, accepting God's promises for them and their children. The major turning point in the story of Exodus is when they don't—when they don't follow God's commands; when they don't recognize God.

Knowing who God is proves a difficult task. Six times prior to the golden calf, God warns them about misidentification. It is the first of the Ten Commandments: "I am the Lord your God, who brought you out of the land of Egypt, out of the house of slavery; you shall have no other gods before me" (Exodus 20:2–3). Remember this commandment? It is not simply a rule but also a promise that the identity of God's people is forever found in relation to God. Forgetting the commandment is infidelity to God. "You shall not make cast idols" (Exodus 34:17). Five more times in the Book of the Covenant (20:22—23:33)—all of the chapters of laws in the book of Exodus, the Hebrews are warned not to get confused about the one true God.[3]

It is surprising to me who does and who does not recognize God in the story of Exodus. At times, certain characters will have a flash of recognition. The first to recognize God are the midwives Shiphrah and Puah. Pharaoh's magicians also recognize Yahweh as the God of the Hebrews. Pharaoh, too, knows that this is the God of Moses and even asks about God's identity, "Who is the Lord?" (Exodus 5:2). Up to this point in the story, prior to the golden calf incident, Yahweh repeatedly asserts to the Hebrews, "I am the Lord," the God of your ancestors. Moses claims a relationship to "our God" (Exodus 8:10). But the Israelites never say! The only time they shout out in apparent recognition of the deity is when they clamor to Aaron to provide them an idol to worship, an occasion fueled by anxiety about Moses's delayed return from Mt. Sinai. This is a turning point for God's people.

---

1. Exodus 3:7; 7:4, 26; 8:16; 9:1, 13; 10:3; 19:6; 20:2–3; 29:46.
2. Exodus 8:18–19; 9:4, 26; 10:23b; 11:7.
3. Exodus 20:22; 22:19; 23:13, 24, 32.

After the dust has settled—and there is much horrendous bloodshed to arrive at this point—neither Israel's nor God's identity is questioned any longer. Before worshiping the golden calf, they were unaware of and unsure of their identity and God's identity. Afterwards, there is no doubt they belong to God. It is settled, and the people faithfully carry out the instructions God has given them—at least in the book of Exodus. They are unequivocally God's people, bound by covenant with God. They have been changed.

The golden calf incident is also a turning point for God. Did you know that God can and does change? Recall the story in the New Testament when Jesus was challenged by the Syrophoenician woman to show love to her, rather than treat her like a dog (Mark 7:24–30). In that encounter, Jesus was changed. In the golden calf passage in Exodus, God is also changed. In response to Moses's plea for the people, God changes God's mind. God repents, turns from wrath, and forgives the people (Exodus 32:14).

This is a remarkable revelation: God can change. So many of us were taught about "the unmoved mover," the platonic ideal of an unchanging, perfect God who is the same yesterday, today, and tomorrow. However, that picture of God needs refinement. God is perfect, but not in the sense of being static, immobile, and unchanging. God's identity is unchanging: God is love. God is also all-powerful, meaning God has the power to change, to grow in relationship, to love actively and to become emotionally involved with us. I believe that God is full of compassion. To have feelings for someone is to be willing and able to be changed in the encounter. To love is to be vulnerable enough to risk being hurt when someone betrays that love. Paul tells us in Philippians that Christ, "though he was in the form of God, . . . emptied himself, taking the form of a slave . . . [and] humbled himself" (Philippians 2:6–8). I believe that when we suffer, God shares in our suffering. I believe that when we are unfaithful, God feels that hurt deeply. We worship a loving God, a self-emptying Christ, not an unchanging idol.

We continually experience turning points in our faith journey as we learn to recognize each other in relationship to God. God recognizes us as God's children, as the people of God. As the people of God at Grandview, we have tried faithfully to express God's love for all persons, inviting everyone into relationship with God, who knows us better than we know ourselves. Kirstin Shrom-Rhoads shared this with me: "When we had [our young children] baptized, we wanted to be in a faith community in which all people are loved and included. A big part of 'all' that is often excluded in the church are people who identify as LGBTQIA+. We wanted our kids to grow up being taught that God's love is NOT exclusive." Another member with young children concurs, "That's why we are grateful to have found Grandview UMC. Its stance as a Reconciling Congregation nurtures the faith we share and want to extend to others."

This unfettered love, this radically inclusive relationship, changes us. Grandview member Morgan Lapp recently shared a testimony by her brother Bill (with his permission), who is married to a man (see quote, above, by William McNavage). Bill was so inspired after a visit to Grandview for a family baptism that he was moved to share his thoughts via Facebook. Here, a self-described non-religious person being inspired to witness publicly to what he experienced in church! As for me, I recognize this as God's prevenient grace, through the power of the Holy Spirit, touching this man's heart while attending worship here at Grandview. Even someone who is not religious can recognize God in our midst and become an evangelist.

Marge Cumpston, the mother of two gay daughters, offers immense gratitude for this community of faith. She told me that they don't have a coming-out story in their family, as so many gay people do who struggle to claim their sexual identity in the face of other's denial, anger, and judgment. When she asked her oldest daughter about this, she replied, "Mom, neither my home nor my church ever told me anything was wrong [with me]." She grew up in a family and a church in which gay people were affirmed and loved. There's much about this faith community of Grandview that touches people's lives and points to God.

The Rev. Mary Merriman reflects on Grandview's journey:

> It's been difficult at times to hear and sometimes engage in conflict with people in the denomination who don't seem to understand the degree of harm that the Christian church—and other non-affirming congregations—have done to gay, lesbian, bisexual, and transgender people. I'm hoping that this congregation's witness will be useful for creating an understanding of the task ahead for Open and Affirming congregations. . . . [but] we too often act in binary ways. It might seem that we can recant our previous positions rejecting LGBTQIA+ people by taking on a mantle of being Open and Affirming. But there is much more to be done.

There's always more to be done. There is always another journey ahead.

To me, this is where our decision to become a Reconciling Congregation becomes a turning point. It would be too easy to turn this stance of acceptance toward homosexuality into an idol, puffing ourselves up with pride that we have already figured it all out and believing that anyone who disagrees with us is on the wrong side of God. How do we avoid making the identity of being "open and affirming" a barrier to our commitment to "cultivate respectful discussion of [theological] differences among all who seek to love their neighbors"? Even our most faithful efforts to do justice in this world—antiracism campaigns, speaking up for rights of immigrants, voting to become a Reconciling Congregation—these efforts emerge from the fire of our righteous passion as idols if we do not also walk humbly with God, if we forget whose we are.

Turning to God as an open and affirming congregation means that we are open to and affirming of the movement of God's Spirit among us. We are open to explore racism and white privilege. We are open to immigrants and refugees. We are open to new styles of worship, new music, and the wondrous gifts shared by new visitors and members. We are open to the journey of faith in relation to God who challenges us to grow and learn together. I believe the decision to become an open and affirming congregation was made not last year but many years ago when leaders and members decided to listen to each other's differences, to learn from each other, to pray and worship together in ways that invited new experiences of grace, and to invite strangers to join us in this journey of faith. Our identity as the people of God means that God is with us. Of that, we can be assured. Thanks be to God.

REFLECTIONS BY RUTH A. DAUGHERTY

Images of God are not always in concrete, visual entities. Could some actions and perceptions also be images/idols that are worshipped? Can our way of interpreting Scripture, adhering rigidly to doctrines, strictly following church disciplinary requirements, and requiring and judging who is fully accepted in our churches be the essence of our understanding of God? To see a concrete form of God limits who/what God is and makes God in the image we want God to be.

As a child, my "image" of God was a strict, judgmental, punishing older figure of a man. I definitely had the picture of a male who was authoritarian, just as men were supposed to be in families and society. My father, who was a pastor, preached often of God punishing and condemning to hell those who disobeyed the laws and commandments in the Bible. While reading the Bible from beginning to end, as expected in my family,

I became aware of the messages of God's mercy, grace, and redemption of those who had done terrible deeds. Those same persons were the ones portrayed as heroes in the Sunday School lessons.

From my mother, I learned about respecting all persons. During the days of the Great Depression, we lived not far from the railroad tracks near the outskirt of a southern city. Often men would jump off the train at that point and come to our house asking for food. Mother would invite them to sit at the table on our screened-in back porch while she prepared something for them to eat. They were to be treated as our guests. Many of the men were African-American, whom we called "colored." My mother's actions gave me an experience that led me to question the discrimination I encountered in schools, and even in churches, and motivation to work to end racism.

The New Testament tells about the kingdom of God as taught by Jesus. His life and message were about relationships with God and with each other. He taught and lived forgiveness, acceptance of those who were ostracized by society, and love for all of humanity. The actions that Jesus condemned were those that were legalistic, self-serving, and pompous. As I concentrate on the way Jesus lived and acted, I see an image of God. Not a concrete, visual image but God being known through liberating, forgiving, loving, accepting, justice-seeking actions.

Connie Brown: My late husband, Alan, was a co-pastor at that time, and somebody in the congregation said, "Well, I'm going to take my young child out of Sunday School because I don't want this gay man who's been a fourth-grade Sunday School teacher to teach my child someday." Alan said, "Well, how old is your child?" And they said, "Four." Alan said, "Well, let's see how things are going as your child gets a little older and we'll talk again." And they did. By that point we had known this man, who had now formed a new relationship with a male. And he was being loved and nurtured and valued in the church and recognized, and well, people began to see, so he's still the same person he was, just a different partnering. And that family was ready to say, "Sure, my kid can be in his Sunday School class."

11

Easter Proclamation
John 6:25–35

"LOVE TRUMPS ALL" BY ANDREA BROWN

I was going to preach a different sermon today, Thanksgiving Sunday. But then, things began to happen. Chuck and Linda Gaston suddenly learned that there was a mass on her brain. Then we got that call from China. Our beloved Ken Weaber had died; it is hard to even express how very much that hurts. And then a pastor from a nearby church, the Rev. Frank Schaefer, was convicted in a church trial, which, whatever you think of the underlying topic or the outcome, was certainly not a great moment in the life of our denomination. And I realized: what we need right now is not a Thanksgiving sermon but an Easter sermon. So I officially declare today Easter, and we are going to tell some resurrection stories.

I found myself thinking a lot about Easter while sitting with several other Grandview members at Frank's trial on Monday. I was thinking about it a lot because the United Methodist pastor who was acting as the "prosecutor" in the trial encouraged the jury to choose punishment over grace, legalism over love, as he made this appeal to what he claimed was precedent: "Never in its history has the Church allowed love to trump all else."

The other Christians in the room looked at each other like, "Huh?" Because it is clear that *at least once* in Christian history, love trumped all else. In fact, that's why we worship on Sundays, not Saturdays like our ancestors: to celebrate the fact that three days after Good Friday, the darkest day in history, love trumped all else. Every Sunday—not just one in March or April and not just this one in November—is a little Easter. Christian worship is a weekly celebration of the fact that love trumps all. That's the Church's organizing principle. It's our most central belief—the truth toward which we orient our lives.

Of course, it is not hard at all to name times when the church failed to live up to the example of Christ—when, indeed, we let other things trump love: the crusades, the inquisition, sectarian fighting in Northern Ireland, slavery in the U.S., genocide of Bosnian Muslims at the hands of Serbia's "Christians," and the slaughter of Native Americans at the hands of a well-known Methodist leader.[1] But normally when we talk about these events, it is certainly not with any notion that we should do more of the same! It is with deep regret. It's a confession: sometimes, we acknowledge, the church has allowed other things to trump love. Lord, have mercy on us. However, at the trial, the statement was made not as a confession but as an encouragement to the jury to keep the precedent: whatever you do, don't let love trump all else. Let rules and regulations trump love.

Can you see why so many of us were scratching our heads and saying, "Huh?" No matter how we feel about homosexuality or same-sex marriage, most of us understand that we follow a Christ who constantly challenged our human tendency to choose rules—cultural, religious, or otherwise—over love.

Should you heal on the Sabbath? Yes, Jesus said: Love trumps all.

Should you eat with tax collectors and other sinners? Yes, he said: Love trumps all.

Should you help an injured man by the side of the road even if it will cause you to break certain rules in your religion? Yes, he told us: Love trumps all.

And then he demonstrated it by giving up his own life. Betrayal? Terror? Death? He was willing to accept these things because love trumps all.

And by God's grace, we *have* seen love trump all in Church history. Right here, even, in the history of this one church, Grandview United Methodist. Right now, we're reaching out to help a family, despite the fact *and because of the fact,* that their son seems to be responsible for the death of an innocent woman and three of her four young children. We also sent

1. On the last point, see Roberts, *Massacre at Sand Creek.*

a gift to the woman's family. Why would we do these things? Because love trumps all.

Each year, Grandview members pledge and give hard-earned dollars to help neighbors and strangers have food to eat, medicine to fight diseases including malaria, and pastors to pray with them when they are sick. We could spend those dollars on ourselves and our families, but we give some away because love trumps all.

A few weeks before Election Day, just when strife in Congress was reaching its boiling point, I found a Republican and Democrat sitting together in our Gathering Space. And I thought, well isn't that just church? He—Glenn Walz—was helping her—Brenda Kauffman—prepare for a debate in her run for office. Why was he doing it? (You know the reason.) Because love trumps all.

Could it really be possible that people can overcome spiritual alienation, the brokenness of sin, the trauma of their past amidst the grace of a loving congregation? Yes! We are blessed to know that love trumps all.

I was awestruck to hear Linda Gaston recount a conversation she had with her twelve-year-old grandson, as she prepared him for her brain surgery. Anyone who knows Linda knows how she feels about her grandkids! Yet she was able to say to him: "It will be fine. And if it is not fine, it will still be OK." Brave words, and she was able to say them because she truly believes that love trumps all.

Ken Weaber, you might say, was the poster child for this truth. Our jobs—our careers—mean a lot to us. They tend to define who we are—our very identity—and maybe especially so for men. But when Ken was forced into early retirement, he didn't shrivel up or let the loss of his career beat him down. Instead, by God's grace, he became even more fully Ken. He became a full-time mission machine, rebuilding homes and lives all over the U.S. and the Caribbean after hurricanes and tornados—homes and people bent down by the chronically weak economy of places including Haiti and Appalachia. He went on over three dozen mission trips. He helped people overcome their own disasters, and in so doing he overcame his.

Love trumps all. No wonder his influence was so great.

I think of all the young people from our congregation whose lives he influenced by his willingness to spend a week with them each year at Appalachia Service Project. I think of his camaraderie with another Ken we met on one of those trips, the two of them reciting epic poetic tales to the delight of all around them. I think of all the kids who know a little more about themselves and their world because of Ken's volunteer work with the Lancaster Science Factory. I think of all the strangers whose day was made at the Pennsylvania Renaissance Faire when they met Ken playing Bacchus, giver of wine and merriment.

I'm so, so, so sad about losing him; I know you are, too. It leaves a gaping hole in our hearts and in our congregation. And yet every time I recall him, the memory brings a smile to my face. And there is no doubt in my mind: Love trumps all.

Our Scriptures today—the ones the lectionary chooses for Thanksgiving Day—speak of manna in the wilderness—the bread that appears out of nowhere. The bread that came to our ancestors despite their complaining and without any effort on their part. It was provided.

Jesus reminds those around him that it wasn't *Moses* who gave them the bread; it was God. Still today, daily, *daily!*, we are being given the bread we need. In the crisis of the present, we look to the past to find hope for the future. For we have all passed through days without bread—if not literally, then metaphorically. Days when we could not see God. The African-American poet Langston Hughes, struggling with persistent discrimination in the middle of the last century, penned the poem "Freedom," which Liz Fulmer pointed out to me the other day. It says in part: "I cannot live on tomorrow's bread."[2] When Liz heard those words, she thought of words from the Lord's Prayer: "Give us this day our daily bread." We are invited by Jesus to ask for bread each day—not to wait for tomorrow, but to expect it and hope for it each day. Living water. Daily bread.

At the end of our Gospel lesson, Jesus tells the people around him, "I am the bread of life. Whoever comes to me will never be hungry, and whoever believes in me will never be thirsty" (John 6:35). He makes the extraordinary statement that there is something more substantial and lasting than anything else—something even more basic than the basics—something that can sustain us even when we are at rock bottom.

A couple from our church went to an adoption ceremony last week for a sixteen-year-old relative. When she was much younger, this girl was repeatedly sexually assaulted by her mother's boyfriend. After years of persistence, the girl's grandparents were finally able to adopt her. And because she has now been living in their household for several years, and because they have been constant in their gentle efforts to help her, she has begun to heal from her devastating past.

2. Hughes, "Freedom [1]," 289.

The other day, someone in school made a rude remark about her body, saying she was too fat to wear the jeans she had on, a brand favored by most teenagers. The implication was that she did not deserve to wear them. But instead of crumbling in the face of the insult, she turned and said to her tormentor, "Someone loves me, and I love myself. And that's why I'm wearing these jeans."

In her life, love has won. In the end, love, our daily bread, will not leave us hungry. For we have been adopted by God. We are children of Love. And if one thing is true, it is this: Love trumps all.

REFLECTIONS BY RUTH A. DAUGHERTY

I walked into the recently dedicated chapel at United Theological Seminary in Dayton, Ohio, and was entranced by the depiction of art in the chancel area. Three panels behind the altar communicate the awesomeness of the Trinity. At the apex of the first panel is the hand of God from which streams a broad beam of light representing the beginning of life. The second panel is a cross, formed from three upright, irregularly shaped branches and two branches as the cross bar. Through the twisted dark forms, light can be seen symbolizing God seeing us through the cross and humanity seeing God through the cross. The instrument of death cannot entirely extinguish life—a reminder of John 1:5: "The light shines in the darkness, and the darkness did not overcome it." The third panel has a dove with wings spread wide with a broad band of light streaming down to the earth representing the Holy Spirit and continuing life.

The light coming through the gnarled branches fascinated me. For me, the cross has always symbolized death. In the artist's depiction of the instrument of death, God, creator of light and life, is still present. Light penetrating the twists and turns of the branches is a harbinger of resurrection—continuing life.

I was reminded of an event involving light during World War II. There were nights when there was to be complete blackout. Dark green blinds covered our windows and we were careful that there were no holes or small cracks through which light might escape. Not even a pin point of light was allowed because that bit of light could be seen if an enemy airplane were to fly over our town. Although no light could be seen from the exterior, there was still light inside.

This is a parable for me in situations when I am involved in struggles for justice, and there seems to be no potential for change. This is particularly true when working for human rights for LGBTQIA+ persons in civil society and the church. Darkness of spirit prevails at times. Then, I recall the image of the light coming through the cross, reminding me of God's presence and the hope of new life abundant—resurrection.

TESTIMONY BY MARY MERRIMAN

On March 19, 1994, I had a heart attack. It was most likely related to stress, poor nutrition, smoking, fasting for ten days prior to the attack, and shoveling snow out of the church parking lot following a big snowstorm. I recovered well from the attack, but later in the year I had another blockage in my heart. I had no insurance. I was earning less than the federal poverty level, qualifying me for Pennsylvania Medical Assistance. What a wake-up call!

I was forty-five years old and had failed in the stewardship of my body that God gave me to care for. I had no retirement funds and was being told I might have only a year to live. In that context, I made the decision to leave Vision of Hope MCC and pursue a master's degree in social work. Initially I thought the MSW degree would enable me to provide counseling within a local MCC, but that vision didn't come to fruition. I made the decision to retire from active ministry in MCC.

God has a sense of humor! Years later, I searched many Lancaster churches—all open and affirming congregations—for a community and place in which my spouse, Ruth, and I could again engage our faith. I visited at least half a dozen or more churches but didn't find the mix of theology, polity, spirituality, and community that I desired. I learned of an inter-faith group called Embrace working to educate mainstream congregations about LGBTQIA+ and to call for full inclusion in religious groups. I attended a couple of meetings and discovered many of the members were from Grandview UMC, which was within walking distance from our home. At that time, Grandview was not known as an open and affirming congregation and the Methodists were having significant conflict regarding the acceptance of LGBTQIA+ people. But seeing the witness of Grandview members and knowing a bit about the associate pastor, I decided to put aside my objections and see for myself.

Ruth remained at home while I attended the worship service. Because I was "out" to many people in the Lancaster area, I was a bit apprehensive that I might meet fire and brimstone. I had no sooner entered the doors, however, than I sensed God's grace pouring out on me in abundance. In the Gathering Space, members and friends of Grandview shared a generous greeting of welcome, as did the ushers and greeters in the narthex and in the Sanctuary. I sat through the worship service and afterward was greeted by Pastor Andrea Brown, who then introduced me to her mother, Connie Brown. I shared my journey with them and they shared their aspirations for becoming a Reconciling Congregation with me. Andrea also shared changes that were in process. The senior pastor, Michael Alleman, would be retiring, necessitating changes in staffing. Andrea, who was familiar with my work as a pastor and social worker, said that I have a combination of gifts that would be valued at Grandview and invited me to worship there again. I returned home and shared what I had received with Ruth, who then decided she needed to see this for herself. We both began attending Grandview weekly.

Ruth and I made an appointment with the pastors. Both were very gracious and affirming as Ruth and I talked openly about our relationship and our successes and struggles in ministry while serving at Vision of Hope MCC. Each of us shared our individual stories about our families and faith backgrounds. I had known Pastor Andrea's dad, the Rev. Alan Brown, when he was a co-pastor at Otterbein United Methodist Church. Two members of Otterbein, Earl Custer and Don Mowrer, were founding members of Vision of Hope MCC. Earl had served as a lay pastor during two Vision of Hope interim periods between pastors.

We then discussed the denomination's stance on homosexuality. I sensed that these pastors were deeply committed to the acceptance of LGBTQIA+ people. They told us that they have been sharing their beliefs in Grandview's membership classes for some time. Each had a personal journey with a friend, colleague, classmate, or family member that undergirded their beliefs. Above all, they had studied and searched the heart of God, which led them in their convictions of acceptance. They explained the process by which the United Methodist Social Principles had been amended years ago and the current inconsistencies. Our meeting was truthful, at times emotional, and profoundly influential in our decision to join Grandview UMC. Ruth and I had found our church home! More likely, the Holy Spirit had called us once more.

Nineteen years after my ministry journey beyond MCC began, I was hired by Grandview United Methodist Church to provide visitation support and assistance for elders who are negotiating the difficult task of aging when illness and infirmities create barriers to participation in the congregation. I also provide support for worship and other activities within the congregation. Once more, I've become very active in advocacy for LGBTQIA+, helping to build the Grandview Reconciling Ministry and exploring the length and breadth of what it means when we say that we are an "open and affirming" congregation.

I was invited to join the Reconciling Ministries Team—a group of members and friends of Grandview interested in helping the congregation to become a Reconciling Congregation. The team provided information on the reconciling process, led discussion groups—including the adult Bible study to examine the ramifications and answer questions about becoming a Reconciling Congregation, wrote the statement that would be published as Grandview's acceptance of LGBTQIA+, and assisted in the voting process. Once Grandview became a Reconciling Congregation, the team continued to work on building the infrastructure in which LGBTQIA+ might find a thriving ministry of support and acceptance at Grandview.

I was apprehensive during my first meeting with the Reconciling Team. Sometimes, even in the midst of support, being a minority can be lonely, as Grandview is largely non-gay. One of my roles was to talk about my experience in ministry with the adult Searchers class. I was nervous about what to expect as a reception in the class. I was thankful for the courteous and forthright discussion, but I tried to be honest in that environment. Even a Bible study group, as it was largely among non-gay people, was somewhat frightening. I used the term "feeling safe" to describe acclimating to the congregation and learning to trust the people. How deeply did they care about the congregation, all of its people, the denomination, and the struggle that LGBTQIA+ are experiencing? I shared a couple of binders of newspaper clippings of my work in civil rights for LGBTQIA+ in Lancaster as well as articles about purchasing our church property in Mountville, Pennsylvania.

I've discovered that I'm continuing to heal from past trauma as a civil rights advocate, a woman, and an LGBTQIA+ person of faith living in a hostile Christian environment. On one Sunday, Dorothy Garboczi best represented the care and grace of Grandview as she tapped me on the shoulder during worship (she was sitting behind me) and asked, "Are you feeling safe yet?" She said, "Give it time, you'll get there." She was right! I continue to grow in my faith in God and trust of others who are different from me, both in lifestyle as well as belief.

ACT V

Setting Out on a New Journey

"I was there twenty-one years. It takes time to change the DNA of a congregation. It's not going to happen in five or six years. It takes a journey together."

—the Rev. Michael Alleman,
on bringing Grandview to a vote to become a Reconciling Congregation

"These doors are always open. We know that it's not about what's written in books; it's about people, and people are welcome here and they're embraced. And that makes a big difference to me."

—Marge Cumpston, member of Grandview

Setting out on a new journey can be daunting. What dangers will we face? What if we fail? What if we succeed?? Continually searching for God and actively listening for the Holy Spirit as we set out can make the difference between remaining lost in the wilderness and entering a promised land.

We are in the midst of great social change in the U.S. and around the world. Sexuality and marriage have been major issues in political discourse for many generations, and the past fifty years have been no exception. In my lifetime, we've moved from the criminalization of homosexual behavior and considering it symptomatic of a psychiatric disorder to understanding the complexities of gender identity and asserting a constitutional right to same-sex marriage. All of this has happened with great speed, and it is difficult for us to keep up. Yet, the need for change was urgent.

At the same time, we are each at different points in the journey. Some of us have not been treated well in church. The so-called "clobber verses" from the Bible that people have used to denounce homosexuality and justify exclusion have left deep wounds. Ironically, one of these—the sin of Sodom (Genesis 19), which through centuries of misguided exegesis lends its name to a sexual act—is interpreted differently in the Bible itself. The sin of Sodom was actually a failure of hospitality and justice for the stranger: they "did not aid the poor and needy" (Ezekiel 16:49). Careful exegesis aside, the story of Sodom has been used to justify hate and condemnation of LGBTQIA+ persons, in much the same way that the story of Ham (Genesis 9:20–27) has been used to justify slavery and racism. The Bible has been used as a weapon of injustice all too often. For persons who have experienced spiritual abuse or abandonment—because they or someone they love is gay, lesbian, bisexual, or transgender—healing takes time.

The church is on a journey in this social wilderness. Whether we are worshipping the golden idol of cultural accommodation or building a new tabernacle to the God of our ancestors—this is a judgment that is most accurately made in retrospect. What I do know, though, is that the people of Grandview have experienced grace in their lives and witnessed the presence of the Holy Spirit in their efforts to extend and recognize God's love with and among LGBTQIA+ Christians. In this book, we have shared "what we have heard, what we have seen with our eyes, what we have looked at and touched, with our hands, concerning the word of life" and "we declare to you what we have seen and heard so that you also may have fellowship with us; and truly our fellowship is with the Father and with his Son Jesus Christ. We are writing these things so that your joy may be complete" (1 John 1:1–3). During the time of immense social change, we can do nothing more important than pray, worship, and fellowship with each other as we discern the word of life that God would have us hear.

And then, we must live by the New Covenant and proclaim the truths we have learned: "And this is his commandment, that we should believe in the name of his son Jesus Christ and love one another, just as he has commanded us. All who obey his commandments abide in him, and he abides in them. And by this we know that he abides in us, by the Spirit that he has given us" (1 John 3:23–24). We do not say this to boast but rather to witness to the faith that has brought us this far and that will continue to guide us as we set out on this new journey. It is a journey of discovery, discernment, and difficulty, and we make this report to you in the midst of the journey. For those suffering, change cannot happen soon enough. This journey requires patience and a sense of urgency.

Thus, this final act dwells on the cross instead of the resurrection. It does not wrap up the narrative in a tidy package, having arrived at the Promised Land. It does not assert final victory, for that belongs to Christ alone. Instead, in chapter 12, "Glimpses Ahead," Michael Alleman offers "The View from Mount Nebo," a sermon about Moses looking out onto the Promised Land that he himself will never reach, a view Alleman compares to his own view onto a congregation that he will no longer lead after his upcoming retirement. Ruth Daugherty reflects on her own "mountaintop experience," and Marge Cumpston tells about the child her daughter and partner adopted.

In chapter 13, "Good Friday," Andrea Brown provides an account of responsibility and refuge, telling the story of a modern day refugee seeking religious freedom in a hostile political and theological environment. Ruth Daugherty reflects on a visit to the Presbyterian Church in Taiwan, a church that committed to a journey of promoting human rights. Mary Merriman shares about Grandview's journey of becoming open and affirming and the grace she's experienced celebrating the sacrament of Holy Communion at Grandview. Act V concludes with an extended conversation among now-familiar Grandview voices. Setting out, we offer not answers but an invitation to join us in the journey ahead.

12

Glimpses Ahead
Deuteronomy 34:1–8

"THE VIEW FROM MOUNT NEBO" BY MICHAEL I. ALLEMAN

The Exodus story extends across the books of Exodus, Leviticus, Numbers, and Deuteronomy. So, it's really the Scripture lesson from Deuteronomy that is the end of the Exodus story, or right near the end of the Exodus story. In it, we hear how Moses gets to look into the Promised Land from Mt. Nebo but will not walk into the Promised Land himself. He does not set foot in the Promised Land at all. You might be thinking, "Well, why is that?"

In the twentieth chapter of the previous book, Numbers, the Israelites were thirsty, thirsting for water. They came to Moses, griping, "We are going to die of thirst out here in the desert. We've come all this way just to die!" Moses goes to God and says, "What am I going to do with these people?" And God says to Moses, "I want you to gather the elders and all the Israelites around this rock and then I want you to tell that rock to bring forth water." So, Moses, following the direction of God, takes his staff, gathers the elders and all of the people of Israel around this rock and then Moses says, "Listen you rebels, shall we bring forth water for you out of this rock?" (Numbers 20:10b). And he takes his staff and hits the rock hard two times—BAM! BAM!—and water comes pouring out of the rock, enough for the Israelites and their livestock as well.

But God says to Moses, "Because you did not follow what I told you to do—you called the Israelites 'rebels' and you struck the rock with your rod, with your staff—you will not enter into the promised land. Because what you've done is you have made it look as if the water coming forth from the rock was something you did, not something I did."

That's a slight shift, just a small shift, and for that he doesn't get to enter into the Promised Land? Well, it's a pretty major shift, from "this is something you have done, Moses, to this is something that I have done through you, Moses," implies God.

It's a mischievous notion for us to think that every generation will get better and better and become more and more like the people God created us to be until finally, in time, we will be God's people. To quote the infamous Dr. Phil: "How's that working for ya'?" Yeah. The truth of the matter is that we grow closer to God living in this balance of discipline—letting our yes be yes and our no be no—the discipline of living out what we speak and speaking what we live out. Surrender. Letting go. Having open hands to receive God's grace and love and all of God's gifts coming to us. This balance has to be here: discipline and surrender. I think it's a piece, a piece of why Moses only gets to view the Promised Land from Mt. Nebo. But I think there are some other pieces to it as well.

I have a pastor friend who retired a little while ago. I wasn't at his retirement celebration, but someone reported back to me that he said he was disappointed because he had always thought that the kingdom of God would come while he was still pastor. Now, I don't think, knowing Frank the way I know him, that he expected the second coming of Christ. I think what he meant is that we would become God's people, kingdom-people, while he was still pastor. Well, I'm just sharing with you that that's not going to be the song I'm singing when I retire. It has nothing to do with any of you. It's not that I'm thinking, ". . . as if the kingdom of God's gonna come while working with a bunch of turkeys like this." That's not at all what I mean. It's about me. My experience is that I only ever capture a glimpse of God, and by the time I turn and focus on God, it's gone. Just this glimpse is all I ever seem to capture.

This past Thursday we had our first choir rehearsal of the season, with thirty members. Oh, it's going to be a tremendous year! I can't wait! During choir rehearsal, I talked to a couple of choir members about something I learned when I was in ninth grade. This was something I *really learned*, not just memorized. Somehow, I was able to make it a part of who I am—that's true learning. What I learned was about the eye, that the eye has cones and rods. The cones are located near the very center of the eye and they are responsible for our ability to see different colors and to see things clearly. The rods allow our peripheral vision, capturing light a whole lot better than the cones do, just by their nature. Did you ever see the commercial on TV where they say, "you can actually see a candle in darkness from six miles away"? I wondered if this was really true.

Because of the earth being round, if you stand up on a mountain and look into the dark, you can see a single candle from thirty miles away. If you're down level, it's only ten miles. A lot of people can see a candle in the dark only one mile away—but even so, a mile away! Back to the commercial—they always end this commercial with a woman looking at a candle in the dark. She's focusing right on it, and I want to say: "No, no, no! You're never going to see it that way. You've got to have your head turned. It's your peripheral vision that will see that candle. That's why they teach the sailors to always be scanning the ocean because you're going to catch it from your peripheral view, not your cones. Your rods are going see that candle. You've got to be moving your head. Your peripheral vision can do this—it's the peripheral vision that gives you the fleeting glimpse."

That's not a bad image of what happens to us with God. We catch a glimpse of God and turn and can't see. So, we turn away, but then we catch a glimpse again. It's there! I know it was right there! That's been my experience when it comes to God's presence in our midst. Some have suggested that this is true because God is always in the becoming. This creating God is always just in the becoming. Others have suggested it's true because when we capture a glimpse, we turn and want to capture God. We want to grab hold of God and nail God down—"This is God!" But remember what God said to Moses in the burning bush. When Moses asked, "What is your name?" God said, "I AM WHO I AM. I WILL BE WHO I WILL BE. You will not box me in with a name or make me something to own. I AM WHO I AM."

So, I never really expected to see God's arrival or the arrival of God's kingdom during my career in ministry, but I always expected that I would be pointing to it. I always expected I would be looking, pointing to God's way, God's kingdom, God's realm, what it means to be kingdom-people.

About twenty years ago, I attended a leadership conference. We were all learning how to write mission statements. Remember when mission statements were the big thing? Here at Grandview we put together a mission statement that has served us very well, that through God's grace we might "help make gentle a bruised world." It's been a great mission statement for us. But you know, it might be time for us to revisit that mission statement in light of what it means for us to be Grandview, today. Anyway, at that conference, one of the things that they had us do was write our own mission statement for our own lives.

Oh, I hated that exercise! It's like someone saying, "Be creative!" Ha, you can't be creative when someone points to you and says, "Be creative. Write your own mission statement." Mumbling, I wrote something down and this is what I came up with: "To be the finger that is always pointing to the one who makes the leaves dance." Yeah, that's ambiguous enough. I can live with that one, I thought: "to always be the finger pointing to the one who makes the leaves dance." Of course, I was really reaping from the Scriptures, that God is like the wind: you do not know where it comes from or where it's going. I was drawing heavily from that. But here's Moses and his view from Mt. Nebo, into the Promised Land, a land that's been promised to Abraham, to Isaac, to Jacob, and all of their descendants. And God says to Moses, "I have let you see it with your eyes, but you shall not cross over there" (Deuteronomy 34:4b).

I tend to think that that might have been almost enough for Moses—not only to have captured a glimpse of but also to see the Promised Land, the Promised Land that for generations had only been a promise. Now, to see it, with his own eyes! I believe that really most of us will walk in Moses's shoes, capturing only a glimpse of this promised land from time to time. When we turn, it'll be gone again, but we capture that glimpse. If it was there and we could stare at it and hold it, then it wouldn't be faith.

Faith demands that it can always be questioned. If it cannot be questioned, then whatever you have, it's not faith. Through faith, we'll capture a glimpse of this promised land and what it means to be kingdom-people, what it means to be part of God's ways. Maybe we'll taste it and drink what it's like. If this seems like a rather large vision or really high goal to set for yourself, I think it's good to have a large goal, a big goal, a God-sized goal, a goal that might be so big that you can't quite capture it, a life-transforming goal. That's the kind of goal that I really want in my life. And if I can't reach that goal, then my hope is that I will have hoisted up someone else to stand on my shoulders, someone who now will have a better view of the goal.

In light of all this imagery, and in light of all that's happened in Ferguson, Missouri, I'm reminded of the late Martin Luther King Jr.'s sermon, "I See the Promised Land." I remember that this was his last speech, the night before his assassination. Here's what he said:

> Like anybody, I would like to live a long life. Longevity has its place. But I'm not concerned about that now. I just want to do God's will. And He's allowed me to go up to the mountain. And I've looked over. And I've seen the promised land. I may not get there with you. But I want you to know tonight, that we, as a people will get to the promised land. And I'm happy tonight. I'm not worried about anything. I'm not fearing any man. Mine eyes have seen the glory of the coming of the Lord.[1]

I wonder if that's how Moses might have felt. My prayer is that this might be true for all of us, whether we reach our goals or not: that from time to time, we will at least have captured a glimpse of the promised land, of what it means to be kingdom-people, and know that this is where we're headed. I think that would be enough. It'd be enough for me.

REFLECTIONS BY RUTH A. DAUGHERTY

I have had a "mountaintop experience"! As a teenager, one of my favorite pastimes was hiking in the mountains. One day, I determined to reach the top of the mountain that could be seen from my house. I began walking on an old, over-grown, tree-lined lumber trail that soon became an obstacle course of deep ruts, large rocks, and fallen trees. The top of the mountain was obscured making it difficult to determine how much farther I had to struggle to overcome the barriers. Finally, I reached the top and had a marvelous view of the forest and valley on the other side, making me want to continue the journey to that picturesque landscape. Then, I looked back at the mountainside and valley from which I had come. It, too, was a view of the handiwork of nature as the obstacles of the climb were no longer distinguishable but blended together in a scene of beauty.

I determined to continue the journey to that lovely picturesque valley on the other side of the mountain. As I descended the mountain on

---

1. King, "I See the Promised Land," 286.

the other side, I was surprised to encounter similar obstacles that had confronted me on the climb up the mountain. But the journey was worth reaching the destination of the valley, where there was a variety of colorful flowers, shade trees, clear flowing streams of water, tall grasses, and scurrying small animals.

This experience has had a major impact on my life as I have attempted to follow Christ's example and teachings. In working for justice and freedom for all LGBTQIA+ persons, there are obstacles of criticisms, judgments, rejections, condemnations, and litigations that may cause delays and detours. There is need for commitment and persistence and, sometimes, persecution to reach the Promised Land after it is viewed from the mountaintop.

I have been on retreats studying and praying for ways to implement the teachings of Jesus; dialogued with persons of differing views; led in-depth discussion groups; spoken on behalf of full inclusion of LGBTQIA+ persons; encouraged others to speak and write for inclusiveness; joined advocacy groups for full inclusiveness; and participated in Grandview's effort to become a Reconciling Congregation.

As I look back and see the journey already taken to the mountaintop and view the scene on the other side, I am reminded that the journey continues. I may not see the time when all of God's people are able to enter the "Promised Land," but I can do whatever I can now to enable that to occur.

Marge Cumpston: At Willow Valley retirement community, there's a couple who would have been wonderful parents, absolutely wonderful parents, but they were not allowed to adopt because one of them is Catholic and one Protestant. Times have changed. Just four years ago, my daughter Mary and her partner Sue were picked by Adoptions from the Heart to be adoptive parents. To apply, Sue and Mary put their pictures on the internet with a statement about how they run their lives and how they run their family, with Sue's daughter, Melissa. Once approved, they got Georgia Marie right from the hospital. She is just spectacular—the light of our lives. She has a Momma and a Mommy.

13

Good Friday
Matthew 27:1–61

"RESPONSIBILITY / REFUGE" BY ANDREA BROWN

When we read the Friday portion of Matthew's Passion narrative, we may immediately wonder who is really responsible for Jesus's death. The most obvious culprit, of course, is Judas. But he does something no one else does: he actually and immediately repents. He takes the money back to the people who gave it to him, saying: "I did wrong. I betrayed an innocent man. Please don't kill him." That's a rare thing for anyone to say: "I did it—I sinned." Much more typical are excuses or non-apologies: "I'm sorry if you were offended." Judas is much plainer than that: "I did wrong; I betrayed an innocent man."

He reminds me of many parents who deeply regret a mistake that affected their children—like using drugs or losing custody because of a crime or error in judgment. Or those parents who simply realize, now that their son or daughter is grown, that they should have been there more or should have yelled less—or should have used a wee bit less sarcasm or should have . . . . Well, the list can be quite long. There are things you can't take back; the damage is done. But while it may be too late to stop what has been set in motion, perhaps it is possible that in some eternal court of justice, such regrets can be heard and accepted and atoned for and made right. For Judas's sake and for our own, I pray it's so.

So, sure, Judas was the betrayer. He's to blame, but he makes for a lousy scapegoat. The story plainly tells us that *all* the disciples bore responsibility: "One of you will betray me, one of you will deny me, and all of you will desert me," Jesus says. We like to look for scapegoats, but when the wrong is great, the responsibility is usually much more widespread. So, where else should we look?

How about the chief priests, the elders, and the scribes? Are they responsible? Yes. Assuredly. But hear this: there is nothing unique about Jewish leadership being corrupt and co-opted. All religions risk this. The proper focus for Christians is on our own chief priests, elders, and scribes—our own bishops and elders and deacons and scholars. Christian church leaders—lay and clergy—frequently sell Jesus out. Witness the preacher who will take no stand on even the gravest injustice in her own community for fear of offending her best donors. Or witness the tepid church leadership that is satisfied with their impressive numbers, when all the while, the neighborhood around the church is made no better for the church's presence in it.

Ultimately, however, even the religious leaders were not the ones who put Jesus to death. They did not have that power. Only the Roman authorities did. The writer of Matthew, a Jewish Christian writing around the year 90 C.E., paints the Roman governor Pilate and his wife in a flattering light. In Matthew's telling, they recognize that Jesus is at the very least faultless and perhaps even special. Matthew chastises his fellow Jews and perhaps tries to curry favor with the present Roman governors, under whose thumb he and other Christians were still living. So the story downplays the Romans' responsibility. But the truth is, only Rome had the authority to carry out a death sentence. Pilate is the one with the most power in this story. Rome had power and chose to use it to execute Jesus on a cross. And it was Rome's soldiers who dressed Jesus up as a king, who flogged him and mocked him and nailed him to the cross.

But how about the people? Weren't they the ones choosing Barabbas? Weren't they the ones yelling, "Crucify him!"? It's essential that we understand that Jewish people as a whole were not and are not responsible for Jesus's death. The misuse of the crowd's words—"his blood be on us and on our children" (Matthew 27:25)—as an anti-Semitic rallying cry is one of the great sins of Christianity. Just two days ago, at a high school basketball game in Massachusetts, students from a Catholic boys' school taunted their opponents from a mostly-Jewish public school with the horrific "cheer," "You killed Jesus."[1] So we know this remains a problem among Christians. The sin is alive.

The vast majority of the people who greeted Jesus on Palm Sunday weren't even aware of what was going on in Pilate's palace on Friday. No one sent them a text message: "Rally at Pilate's at 1 p.m. today." A large crowd wouldn't have fit in Pilate's courtyard. Marcus Borg and John Dominic Crossan argue persuasively that the crowd yelling "Crucify him!" must have been quite small—nothing like the massive throngs who greeted Jesus on Palm Sunday.[2] Most of them would have been working that day—nowhere near Pilate's house. And if they would have known about it—and if they could have gotten there—they might well have tried to stop the disaster—to keep protecting the man they saw as a folk hero if not the actual messiah.

The small, Friday crowd was likely brought and bought by the corrupt religious leaders to help them bolster their case to the Romans. Only by applying significant pressure and propaganda were and are authorities ever able to co-opt the people, who sometimes don't even know what is happening in their name because it is intentionally hidden from them. The same happens today. Think of covert actions carried out by the U.S. government at the behest of certain business interests, which the people did not knowingly bless. And yet at some level, we *are* still at fault.

Indeed, we do bear some responsibility even when things we don't know about happen in our name. We might not be standing in the streets yelling "Crucify him!" but we *do* participate in Jesus's crucifixion when we repeat lies and rumors, when we mock or belittle others, when we treat some as "less than," when we support candidates who justify torture of "foreigners" who aren't foreign to Jesus. We bear responsibility for not knowing or remembering our own history.

* * *

Grandview has a long history of resettling refugees that began during the Vietnam War. Since then, we have resettled about a dozen families fleeing war and extreme ethnic persecution. And some war refugees, like our members from Liberia, have found their way to us on their own. The stories

1. Rios, "Anti-Semitic Taunts." This, of course, is not the only example of anti-semitic behavior by Christians.

2. Borg and Crossan, *The Last Week*, 144.

are harrowing. In one family we resettled, the dad had to sneak out at night, under cover of darkness, to try to get food for his starving family. The exploding ordnance around him was his only light, so he would run a bit each time a bomb would explode, lighting up the forest floor for him. In those perilous conditions, he once disappeared for several days. Meanwhile his wife and children back at home did not know whether he was dead or alive. That was a devastating and heartbreaking thought for them but it was also a matter of their own life and death.

At what point should the mother send out her oldest son, as well, to try to bring back some food before she and his little brother and sister all starved to death? How many members of their family would they have to sacrifice? And can you even imagine having to make such a decision? Eventually, she did send that son out, and he found his father who had become lost. They were able to bring back a little food and water just as the others were on the brink of death. But the boy was so badly shell-shocked that he had severe PTSD years later—leaping up in terror at any loud sound and suffering crushing headaches and violent outbursts.

A few years ago, other refugees began arriving on our church's doorstep. One was a leader of a Christian group—and indeed Christianity was the majority religion in her home country. But, for tribal reasons, most Christians in that country regarded this woman's group as inferior to them—much as the Jews had viewed the Samaritans as inferior to them, even though the Samaritans thought of themselves as just as Jewish as anyone else. Do you remember when the disciples asked Jesus whether they could call down a bolt of lightning on the Samaritan village and wipe those people out? (For the record, Jesus did not approve of their plan for ethnic cleansing.) Well, that's literally what many of the Christians in this woman's home country were trying to do to her and her tribe.

To show that they, too, were Christian, she and some of the other leaders from the same tribe, wearing their stoles, crosses, and other signs of faith, went on a multi-day prayer walk across a part of the country that was especially hostile to them. They would walk several miles and then stop to pray or to read their Bibles or to talk with people they encountered. They were good-will ambassadors—trying to help people see them as safe, faithful, and non-threatening. But one evening, after they made camp, a group of men drove up in a pick-up truck. Each man was carrying a gun. They told the Christian marchers that if they did not leave by morning, they would come back and shoot them. After prayer, the group's leadership decided that this was not the time for martyrdom. They had many miles to go in giving their witness. So they packed their things into a van and drove to their next campsite, with the pickup's headlights shining in the window. A child who was walking with his parents in the march was told to stay on the floor of the van so that he would not be shot.

On another day, they came to a town they had planned to walk through on the way to their destination in the capital city. The residents of that town, many of them hurling vulgar insults despite the crosses they wore around their necks, tried to block this weary group of pilgrims from entering. Some of the townspeople even picked up stones. Others, the walkers may have feared, probably had guns and knives. The townspeople lined the streets on either side of the preachers as they made their way down the main street. Some in the crowd were merely curious. Others were openly hostile. Some carried signs, written in their language, saying simply, "Die." Others the walkers met along their journey shouted, "God hates you" or "Rot in hell." Our friend was relieved when they made it through to the other side. (I imagine them shaking the dust off their feet, as in Matthew 10:14.)

Later, she moved a few hundred miles away to another part of the country she hoped would be less hostile. But when she and the other members of her tribe began looking for a safe space to meet, the hostility appeared there, too. This was in the early 1990s. A bookstore where the group often gathered was attacked by an arsonist and burned to the ground. No one was ever prosecuted. She received many threats. When she and her congregation tried to find a permanent place to worship together, two dozen local Christian clergy wrote a letter trying to block them. Didn't these clergy see that they were trying to keep people from worshiping Jesus—trying to keep them from sharing the Gospel?!

The town council seemed determined to prevent the tribe from worshiping in that town. But in the end, some townspeople—from a different Christian tribal group—listened with their hearts and minds as well as with their ears, and they could see that this tribe of Christians was sincere in their faith. In the end, the crowd actually agreed to the plans.

So led by God, this pastor and her congregation bravely and prayerfully persisted, even when the other so-called Christian clergy took out a full-page ad against the new church. On the eve of their first worship service in an old church building they scraped together money to buy, they got a call from the regional police, promising protection—a clear reminder of the peril they were in. She, the pastor, was afraid for her parishioners, but they worshiped anyway, putting their lives in God's hands and the hands of those police.

But because of all the stress everyone was under, the tribe became conflicted after a few years, as churches can do. The stressed-out pastor eventually had a heart attack. For many years, even though Christ meant everything to her, she simply could not be in church—any church. She had been hurt so badly and frightened so badly by other Christians, she simply could not be a part of the Church.

But one day that woman—you know her; her name is Mary Merriman—walked in our doors here at Grandview. And here she found refuge. She frequently tells others about how good that feels. But I'm haunted by the story of that prayer walk in Florida and her time of trying to plant a church in Mountville, Pennsylvania, not that long ago and of that bombing of the gay bookstore in Lancaster as recently as the 1990s.

Another refugee walked in our doors a few years ago, too, the former executive director of the local Planned Parenthood clinic. That clinic was firebombed in 1993, presumably by someone who would call himself a Christian, since it is people who call themselves Christians who have committed every *solved* murder and arson at other women's health clinics around the country. The attack in Lancaster was never solved, though; no one was arrested or charged.

Although she has a degree from Boston University School of Theology and has been led by Christ all her life, for years, Nancy Osgood simply could not attend a church. So many Christians had been so ugly to her, she simply could not bring herself to worship among them. What hurt even more was that many *other* Christians were relentlessly *silent* when she and her staff and her patients needed vocal support—when they needed someone to partner with them in saying, "Women's lives matter." But time passed, and God nudged Nancy to find a place of refuge. Here, at last, she did.

Even more recently, a member of our church was informed by *his* Christian bosses that his job would be taken away because he refused to renounce his gay friends and fellow church-goers. Some years back, another man from this congregation gave up a job because he refused to cooperate with his Christian boss's embezzlement from the non-profit for which they worked.

And if we are thinking: "Those crooked, judgmental Christians are not like us; we would never treat people—treat Jesus—the way they do," well, let's remember that the hardest log to see is always the one in our own eye. We are not immune to hurting people, even the ones we love. When I talked about that "whenever you did it/failed to do it" passage a few weeks ago (Matthew 25:31–46), one wise member said afterward, "Did you really have to preach that sermon just to me today?" He was not the only one who could see himself in it—could find himself on the goat side of Jesus's judgment parable sometimes. We all can.

Recently, Mary began recalling another incident from the prayer walk. After they made it through that hostile town in southern Florida, one of the town's preachers followed them, trailed by some of his parishioners. He followed them all the way to the capitol, shouting insults into a bullhorn. When they arrived at the capitol steps, he told his congregation to stone those sinners.

The leader of the prayer walk, who was the head of the Metropolitan Community Church, quietly asked young Mary to walk up on the steps and begin singing a familiar hymn. This made her even more vulnerable to their stones and stares, an even easier and greater target. But as she ascended those steps and began to sing that familiar hymn, she could feel the tension ease. Something about the song, or (I would say) about her courage in standing alone up there singing it—something in the movement of the Spirit—was what finally helped them to see her and the other members of her tribe as Christians just like them. As Mary turned to face the crowd and started singing, she saw the hostile preacher's followers all begin to move away from him. She could see a woman from that church lifting her baby up, as if in affirmation. Some even sang along: "Amazing Grace, how sweet the sound, that saved a wretch like me. I once was lost, but now I'm found, was blind but now I see." For that moment, the danger had ended. Christ had found a way.

Where can God seek refuge in this hostile world? Where can Jesus find a friend who will stay with him? Well, even here in this darkest story ever, the story of that first Good Friday, there are that handful of people who show up or who stay close, at personal risk to themselves. Simon of Cyrene. Joseph of Arimethea. And a couple of women named Mary. And to the rest of us, Jesus offers an unfailing word of grace: "Father, forgive them; for they do not know what they are doing" (Luke 23:34). In the end, our hope is not in ourselves, but only in those spare but wondrous words spoken from the cross: "forgive them."

Forgive us, Lord.

REFLECTIONS BY RUTH A. DAUGHERTY

"What a Good Friday experience!" is the way my journal begins for Friday, March 24, 1978. A visit of our group from the Board of Global Ministries of The United Methodist Church with Dr. C. M. Kao, Secretary-General of the Presbyterian Church in Taiwan, was scheduled for two o'clock in the afternoon at his office in Taipei. It was to be a meeting to learn about the reported persecutions of the Presbyterian Church for its advocacy to guarantee the security, independence, and freedom of the people of Taiwan. After preliminary greetings and introductions, Dr. Kao suggested we go to the coffee shop for refreshments.

Many Taiwanese were in the coffee shop and it was quite noisy. Upon being seated, Dr. Kao explained his office was bugged and we could talk freely in the coffee shop in the midst of all of the clamor without fear of being overheard or recorded. The Presbyterian Church in Taiwan had issued "A Declaration on Human Rights" on August 16, 1977, addressed "To the President of the United States, to all countries concerned, and to the Christian churches throughout the world."[3] The Declaration promoted a new and independent country, requesting that the people who lived there determine the future of Taiwan.

Dr. Kao spoke of the harassment, censorship, and threats to which he and other officials of the church had been subjected as they continued to support the Declaration. Seven months after the adoption of the Declaration, few voices had been heard in support of this church's stance or even in opposition to the persecutions that were taking place. He said the persecution by the government had increased, and he was convinced that he would be arrested and imprisoned. He spoke of the significance of the day (Good Friday) when we were meeting and the meaning it had for him. I remember vividly his final words: "But after the suffering, came the resurrection." I marvelled at the faith and courage that Dr. Kao had shown.

A short time later, Dr. Kao was arrested and sentenced to prison. The Presbyterian Church in Taiwan continued to acknowledge him as the Secretary-General, and when meetings were held, a vacant chair with his name was prominent where the leadership was seated. Dr. Kao was released from prison after several years and actively resumed his leadership.

During the difficult days, the closing words of this Declaration on Human Rights, quoting Psalm 85:10–11, became statements of hope and

3. Presbyterian Church in Taiwan, "A Declaration on Human Rights."

promise for Easter people in the Presbyterian Church in Taiwan: "Mercy and truth will meet together; righteousness and peace will embrace. Truth shall spring out of the earth; and righteousness shall look down from heaven."[4]

TESTIMONY BY MARY MERRIMAN

No one knew what to expect when Grandview finally voted to join the Reconciling Ministries Network (RMN). All congregations celebrate differently. We placed the RMN logos on the outside bulletin board, the mission statement in the bulletin and on the website, and posted the certificate of recognition from RMN on the bulletin board in the Gathering Space. We didn't have a big media blitz or bring out a blaze of rainbow flags. We were very cognizant that we needed time together as a Reconciling Congregation to live out our new mission statement that embraced people with different perspectives.

While I've found great cause for celebration, I also have great cause for pessimism regarding the United Methodist process for inclusion of LGBTQIA+ within the denomination. I've lived through the era of Anita Bryant, Jerry Falwell, and Pat Robertson persecuting LGBTQIA+ in the United States. So, I was saddened to hear some of the same campaigns of misinformation being offered by clergy and laity as LGBTQIA+ demonstrated for change and called for greater inclusion in the denomination's *Book of Discipline*. The United Methodist Church's reluctance to change has affected me personally.

In 1990, I met the love of my life—Ruth Stetter. In 1993, we solemnized our relationship in a service of holy union at Vision of Hope MCC. After the state of Pennsylvania legalized same sex marriage in 2014, we decided to get married. However, The United Methodist Church prohibits its congregations from holding celebrations and its clergy from officiating same-sex weddings. Ruth and I were married in our Lancaster backyard with Ruth's daughters and sons in law, our grandchildren, two of my sisters, our pastors from Grandview UMC, and other friends in attendance. We were blessed to have the same clergywoman—Rev. Arlene Ackerman—officiate our legal wedding ceremony. We joke that we had the longest wedding ceremony as it took twenty-one years to finalize what others had experienced in twenty-one minutes!

4. Ibid.

At Grandview, we continue to develop our conversations regarding the acceptance of LGBTQIA+ through our involvement with Embrace, an interfaith alliance in Lancaster committed to helping faith communities become more accepting and supportive of LGBTQIA+ in their congregations and communities. I, along with other members of Grandview, have worked with Embrace to provide videos on LGBTQIA+ acceptance in the public libraries, participated in Pride Fest in Lancaster and Millersville, participated in school programs, such as the Millersville University Sexuality Conference, and set up a table on the topic of the inclusion of LGBTQIA+ for Solanco School District. With Embrace, Grandview Church co-sponsored the "We're Affirming—Now What?" Conference at Lancaster Theological Seminary[5] and presented the video "From Selma to Stonewall" with Rev. Gil Caldwell during the Eastern Pennsylvania Annual Conference of the UMC in June of 2016. We've also participated in the Transgender Day of Remembrance and World AIDS Day events and National Coming Out Day.

There is a gulf in my heart that longs to be filled, and by God's grace, it is occurring! It's occurring as people like Dorothy Garboczi touch my shoulder and utter a comforting word. I'm reminded that people are listening and caring that I find that healing in their midst in Grandview. It's occurring as parishioners participate in sensitivity training especially recognizing the importance of allowing LGBTQIA+ their space to "come out." It's not necessarily an LGBTQIA+ safe world outside of the safe space of open and affirming congregations. It's occurring every time I have the opportunity to take part in worship. The first Sunday the pastors invited me to distribute communion, I was overwhelmed with the image of non-LGBTQIA+ people coming to receive communion from me, aware that I am a lesbian. While LGBTQIA+ have been demonized and labeled as unfit to receive the blessings of God, that day it was different—full of grace!

Since coming to Grandview and healing in this church over the past few years, I've uncovered a deep, personal relationship with Jesus that I'm relearning to live each day. The song, "For Those Tears I Died," has become emblematic of my relationship with God through Jesus. Marsha Stevens, a lesbian Christian artist and colleague, wrote this song with her former husband. This song was widely embraced. However, after Marsha divorced her husband and came out as a lesbian, many groups stopped performing this piece of music, and churches removed it from their hymnals. I've witnessed

5. See epilogue for "Challenges to Community and Ministry" arising from this conference.

the words of this song being lived out by believers and non-believers, clergy, and laity. While institutions may be struggling, many LGBTQIA+ have found peace in the arms of faith in Jesus and long only to share that peace with others.

To conclude my personal testimony, and in honor of the struggle for religious freedom and the deep spiritual longing of LGBTQIA+ persons throughout the world, I share Marsha Stevens's lyrics:

> You said You'd come and share all my sorrows,
> You said You'd be there for all my tomorrows,
> I came so close to sending You away,
> But just like You promised, You came there to stay,
> I just had to pray.
>
> Chorus:
>
> And Jesus said, "Come to the water, stand by my side,
> I know you are thirsty, you won't be denied.
> I felt every teardrop when in darkness you cried,
> And I strove to remind you, that for those tears I died."
>
> Your goodness so great, I can't understand,
> And, dear Lord, I know that all this was planned.
> I know You're here now, and always will be,
> Your love loosed my chains and in You I'm free,
> But Jesus, why me? (back to chorus)
>
> Jesus, I give You my heart and my soul,
> I know that without God I'd never be whole,
> Savior, You opened all the right doors,
> And I thank You and praise You from earth's humble shores,
> Take me I'm Yours.[6]

GRANDVIEW VOICES: A CONVERSATION

Setting out on a journey of open and affirming ministry involves more than a referendum. The vote to become a Reconciling Congregation was just one part of a journey that began years earlier and will continue for years into the future. The following consists of excerpts from a conversation at Grandview

6. Stevens-Pino, *For Those Tears I Died*, 60–61. Lyrics copyright © 1969 Bud John Songs (ASCAP) (adm. at CapitolCMGPublishing.com) All rights reserved. Used by permission. Bill Gaither's arrangement is available for purchase at http://www.musicnotes.com/sheetmusic/mtd.asp?ppn=MN0059064.

*about what open and affirming ministry means and should continue to mean
for this church as it sets out on the next leg of its journey.*

Marge: I'm very uptight these days about exclusivity. Who are we going to exclude this week? Who is it all right to not love this week? You don't
hear it here, but we go to vespers once a week at our retirement community. One week it's the Muslims that have done something wrong, and the
next week, it's a particular denomination. Last week, the priest was on the
Baptists for some reason or another. There's always somebody mentioned
that it's going to be okay this week if you exclude them. I think we need to
do what we do here at Grandview and preach inclusiveness, because as a
church, we're going to die if we don't do this. We've got to start including
people, not excluding. I'm not sure I understand why it's so important to
exclude. Grandview is inclusive. Grandview loves people, and that means
so much. It's just really critical, in my mind.

Mary: This morning Andrea mentioned in the sermon the concept
of horizontal hostility in the 1970s: groups being pitted against each other.
It's a tool of oppression, but I don't think churches think about that often.
So when I start hearing stuff like the sermons you were hearing, Marge, it
just disturbs me, it really does, that we fail to see that part of God's hand at
work, to bring some unity to creation.

Marge: Lou's brother had no church affiliation when he died. He was
being buried in a military ceremony, which they only do Monday through
Friday. So the funeral director got this young pastor to come and do the
service on a Friday, and he did a very nice job. Since we were there for the
weekend, I said to Lou, "Let's go to his church. We can at least do that." So,
we went to this young pastor's church.

Well, when I go to church, I sit in the middle of the pew because I
don't like people walking on me. So I sit in the middle and leave both ends
open. So that's what we did, and we had people sitting on both sides of us.

"Now today, we're going to discuss a very important topic." It comes
up in capital letters, right in front, "HOMOSEXUALITY." I looked at Lou,
and I said, "Do we really need this?" I was not ready to stay. But we couldn't
get out very easily, so we had to sit there. The young preacher went over
his graduating class, saying, "This one left the ministry and has moved to
England so that he can be who he really is. This one sang at my wedding.
Now he's come out as gay. You know, I'm having to think about this quite a
bit." They'd all been in seminary together.

And you could tell this young man was really working this over in his mind, and I was so glad that we had been forced to stay, to see this preacher going through all of this and struggling with what he'd been taught and with what he knew and what his heart told him. It was a very interesting morning. Someway, somehow, some hand from above stuck us in the right place that morning.

Connie: One of the sermons that sticks in my head from Mike Alleman was one in which he happened to tie in an experience working with the youth in the congregation. I think the topic of the sermon was relationships. There were several teens sitting down in front, and he was telling about a message that he utilized sometimes in sex-education aspects of our youth program, saying to some of the young boys in this instance, "So, what do you think when you meet a new girl? She's just moved into the area."

The boy answered, "Well, you look at her and see what you think of her appearance."

Mike said, "Okay, all right. So, you check out this object." And he said, "So she happens to be at the bus stop at the same time you are. You might ask her, 'What do you like? You like sports, you like music?' You begin to find out some of her interests. 'You like math? You like English?' Then, you're building a relationship."

So, as to sex education: yes, we need to know the mechanics, but to learn the relationship is so vital. I really think so much of our need to say, well our version of religion is the best; or our football team is the best, whatever, is because we have inadequacies within ourselves and we need to feel we're superior to somebody. We've seen that played out so severely in the race issue. The wealthy of the South played the white people against the slaves by putting up a resentment there. It just happens a lot. We have a need for a feeling of community and somebody who will stick together with me, but keep those others on the outside, and "the other" changes over the years.

One time Otterbein Church, here in the city, held neighborhood gatherings, like we've just had at Grandview. We were discussing the issue of sexuality with our peers, and one of the rather conservative fellows in this group of about four couples, said, "Well, you know, I'm not quite ready to accept gays. But, I've been thinking, out of all of these conversations we've had, well we used to be told by the church that divorce was terrible and anyone who was divorced was terrible. But gradually, I began to realize some of my five siblings were divorced. And they weren't any better or any worse than they were before they were divorced people. So, maybe that extends to people of different sexual orientations, too."

Darryl: In the early 1990s, The United Methodist Church put out a study called, *The Church Studies Homosexuality*. I don't know if any of you remember that—a study booklet and report. Our congregation in Houston did a study of this as soon as it came out, so I joined in. I was just out of college at that time. One of the men there, a good old Texas guy, said to the group, "I'm not sure what I think about this, but I do believe that sexual orientation is not chosen. Science tells us that 5–7 percent of people are just born gay or lesbian." And he said, "What I do know is, I want this church to be a place where the youth and children of this congregation who are gay and lesbian will have positive role models and learn what it means to be Christian in this church." That was where he could rest, even with all his personal confusion, in this journey of figuring it out. He loved the children enough to be open to what he did not understand.

Connie: And I thank Mary, especially now, recognizing that I'm the grandparent not only of children who are either bisexual or gay but also trans. Mary's statement this morning, about prayers for transgender persons who are so much at risk, has great meaning.

There's always complexity involved with finding our sexual identity. The transgender issue involves not only stating to the person the orientation but also all these physical things that have to be approached and dealt with. That really, really is an additional challenge, and persons really need additional caring, nurturing, and help through that.

Marge: I like very much the idea that I can be encouraged that the younger generation is going to be a little more open about sexual orientation. But I'm also concerned that the younger generation will have just as many hate-people. There was a big attack in Philadelphia on a gay couple, and it was a bunch of young kids from a local college that did the attacking.

Mary: But the messages are different, and the community group is a little more heterogeneous. There's more likelihood that they've been exposed to things that are positive, as well.

Marge: I hope so. I hope so.

Dorothy: A concern I have is that the part of our clergy that comes from overseas, at General Conference, tends to vote in a very negative way. And yet, as a missionary in Zimbabwe, I saw men walking together hand-in-hand, which I would never see in this country. Women walk hand-in-hand; men walk hand-in-hand. There's no—what we would see as something stigmatized in this country because it's like we were so cut off from being able to express our emotions because of the stigma that it might raise. And I did not see that. So, it's sad that those same people, the ones who are very active have been taught—and many of the missionaries that I worked with were very conservative and judgmental. It's sad that that has been indoctrinated.

Lou: I carry this man-bag, purse, whatever you want to call it. And once in a great while, I've got to be a little careful in the parking lot, when someone points their pickup at me.

Marge: One guy was headed right at him and said, "I've always wanted to hit a guy wearing a purse." A parking lot in Gulf Breeze, Florida.

Lou: The man-bag just carries with it the message: "I'm queer."

Dorothy: And yet in Thailand, men carry their shoulder bag just like women do.

Lou: Well, I used to travel to Europe many times during the course of a year for work. And everybody there is carrying a purse like this, all the males. So, I just felt this was a correct thing to do. It's a whole lot easier on my back than sitting on a wallet all the time.

Andrea: Not only does it signify something here that it doesn't in other cultures, it also makes some people feel like it would be okay or even good to harm you.

Lou: Yes, which is really sad. It's tragic.

Mary: But at the same time, it also gives some people permission to say, "Yes, I can be different, to wear a bag or a purse or whatever you want to call it."

Marge: Somebody just this morning came to look at his man-bag—he's shown it to several people—saying, "Maybe that's what I need to go to Europe. Because it'll hold a tablet. It'll hold everything."

Dorothy: One of my other experiences in ministry... My husband and I followed Gene Leggett and his wife when he moved to Austin, Texas, and we moved to Dilley (half-way between San Antonio and Laredo). Gene had served in Dilley. He was a very talented person—good in drama. Just a very impressive person. Later he came out as gay, and it was so tragic. His final appointment was associate pastor at First UMC in Austin. The Southwest Texas Conference of our church crucified him. When we lived in Bangkok, Thailand, we were shocked to see his name on the front page of the Bangkok paper because he's gay. It's so sad that even the church would be so cruel to people. We lose a lot of good talent because people are discounted because of their life. He was a really neat person. He had three sons. It's sad that he has died. I still have contact with Fanny, his wife, who remarried.

Connie: I think we need, as a church, to figure out how to love people and to actively let them know that they are loved.

Darryl: Anything else on one's heart before we close?

Marge: Back to my immense gratitude. Thank you so much! We're at home; we're okay here at Grandview. I can wear my rainbow stole. I can talk about my kids. Thank you.

"A COVENANT PRAYER" BY RUTH A. DAUGHERTY

A COVENANT PRAYER
O God of the Covenant—
Creator of us all,
Provider for us all,
Divine Lover of us all.
Forgive us—
for our self-centered arrogance,
our conscious and unconscious attitudes of superiority,
our lack of interest and concern for other members
of your family of humanity.
In our faith journey—
open our eyes to see the way;
open our ears to hear your Word;
open our minds to understand what we see and hear
open our hearts to sensitivity to your presence
in our living and in the lives of our neighbors.
In the name of Jesus Christ, the Covenant Incarnate.
AMEN.

Epilogue

Most of us are already on the journey of open and affirming ministry, whether we know it or not. Claiming the journey is a way of reinterpreting the past in a way that conforms to the good future God prepares for us. To recover a Christian voice amid profound social change, particularly regarding sexuality and gender, Christians must continue to draw upon Scripture, tradition, reason, and experience as essential guides to a faith seeking understanding. We must seek God. When we faithfully see ourselves in the biblical narrative, we are not the heroes or saints but the sojourners, the wayward people seeking God even as God has already called us by name. The journey of faith is one of growth in "holiness of heart and life."[1] This journey is about living into the new life born of water and the Spirit and, then, sharing it with others, indiscriminately and generously. The Good News is a story about God's gracious actions in our lives, to which we are both recipients and witnesses.

Read this book with others. Let these stories prompt your memory, stir your passion, and provoke your faithful response. Listen to your fellow travelers as they share their own stories. Feel the presence of God in your midst. Learn anew to recognize the movement of the Spirit. "O taste and see that the Lord is good; happy are those who take refuge in him" (Psalm 34:8). Take nourishment through prayer, fellowship, and worship. The journey ahead is a long one, with many challenges to community and ministry.

Before embarking on an intentional process to become a Reconciling Congregation, Grandview had spent over a decade sowing the seeds of radical hospitality in soil cultivated by the faith of many generations. To

---

1. This is a reference to the Wesleyan theology undergirding this book. See, for example, Yrigoyen, *John Wesley: Holiness of Heart & Life*.

prepare your own faith community to claim this journey, consider what in your congregation's history prepares you for this moment. As a congregation, write a timeline of significant events in your church and community. Share stories about changes in the congregation and how you overcame challenges. Remember and re-narrate your past in light of the future to which God is leading you.

There will be fear. Members may ask, "What if families decide to leave our church?" Business owners in the congregation may wonder, "How will my customers react to this?" Community leaders in the church may fret, "Will I lose votes and political support?" There will be resistance. Not everyone will be comfortable with a public stance of open and affirming ministry. It is likely that some congregants will leave, some customers will go elsewhere, and some voters will protest. However, there are also folks who are waiting for your congregation's unambiguous voice of love and justice before joining and offering their support. Grandview has grown since the vote to become reconciling, and nearly every new member and family says they were drawn to this congregation because of our commitment to open and affirming ministry. Claiming the journey means being clear about who and whose you are. Only then will people know if they are ready to join you in the hard road ahead.

There will be trials. Not long after Grandview became a Reconciling Congregation, we were the target of hate speech and threats. On more than one occasion, an anonymous protester wrote disturbing messages on the sidewalk near the front entrance to the church building, singling out Pastor Andrea.[2] The church responded with justice, prudence, and grace. We called the police to make a report, we increased security in the building and around our pastor, and we proclaimed the Good News for all to see and hear, covering our sidewalk with messages of love in a rainbow of chalk colors.

There will be additional challenges. As Grandview broke down the walls of shame and secrecy about sexuality, we learned to recognize other forms of exclusion more clearly and felt better equipped to talk about them. In a recent sermon drawn from the Gospel of John, Pastor Andrea reflected:

> when this congregation came out as an open and affirming place,
> we began to be able to deal with other sources of shame more
> frankly, too. We talk about money here—that great taboo subject.

2. Grandview is not alone in being targeted for hate speech. See, for example, Crescente, "Clifton Church Vandalized with Sexual Slurs."

We talk about our political differences—which isn't always easy in this climate, but at least there's not a deafening silence. Several people in the last few years have come out about their mental illness, which has de-stigmatized that topic and helped us to overcome ableism that can make people into outsiders. We're now far better able to talk about racism and how it has affected or infected us. . . . Good questions for us to continue to ask are: "What is still hard for us to talk about here? Who is still not welcome?" Because, like some Pharisees, we may still want to resist what God is doing.

As a Christian community, we get stronger as we address additional challenges, gaining not only tools but also a new and renewed sense of identity in relation to God. This journey will change you. Do not expect to remain as you are when God is doing a new thing in your life. You will be transformed.

CHALLENGES TO COMMUNITY AND MINISTRY BY MARY MERRIMAN

When a congregation becomes open and affirming, the usual activities of the congregation might change. Creating and maintaining welcoming practices is an ongoing challenge, requiring sensitivity and training. In 2015, Embrace provided support for a conference in Lancaster, Pennsylvania, entitled, "We're Affirming—What's Next?" The conference explored opportunities for creating ministry with LGBTQIA+ people. Experienced laity and clergy from open and affirming ministries throughout the Mid-Atlantic region participated. The conference provided congregational resources to address challenges to community and ministry in several areas of congregational practice: public and private witness; policy and leadership; and programming.[3]

Public and Private Witness

Personal witness is the most significant way in which LGBTQIA+ people have gained acceptance. Sharing one's own experiences of overcoming oppression and the impact of trauma can promote healing and has a profound impact on the listener. However, it isn't always easy to elicit conversation.

---

3. The following material is adapted from this conference, "We're Affirming—What's Next?" held at Lancaster Theological Seminary on September 19, 2015, co-sponsored by Grandview United Methodist Church, Welcoming Dialogue, and Embrace.

Many congregations don't experience progress in open and affirming ministry until they demonstrate an understanding of the dilemmas that LGBTQIA+ persons face. Many LGBTQIA+ persons have a need for privacy, and all have a right to expect that their anonymity will be protected. How can congregations create safe spaces for LGBTQIA+ persons and allies to share their stories?

Awareness of the social, cultural, and political context is vitally important. Legal protections and rights for LGBTQIA+ persons vary greatly throughout the world. While same-sex marriage is legal in nearly two-dozen countries, homosexual acts are illegal in over five-dozen countries.[4] In the United States, there is a growing list of protected classes that have been assured access to housing, education, employment, and public accommodations through federal and state civil rights law. However, sexual orientation and gender identity are generally not federally protected classes in the United States, and many states have limited legal protections for LGBTQIA+ persons. Individual municipalities may have equal rights ordinances on their books, but those same rights may not be accorded outside the boundaries of the municipality. Day to day living can become very complex. In some adult housing communities, two unrelated adults are required to rent two bedrooms, even if they are a couple. While marriage equality is a national right, in some states, applying for a marriage license will result in having one's name published in the newspaper. If the state does not have legal protections for LGBTQIA+ in housing, education, employment, and public accommodations, disclosure that one is in a same-sex relationship can result in a loss of employment and housing, which may have catastrophic results for one's physical, emotional, and spiritual well-being.

Open and affirming congregations should consider the following with regard to public and private witness:

- Educating congregants on the need for sensitivity to confidentiality;

- Supporting LGBTQIA+ members and allies in telling their stories;

- Supporting LGBTQIA+ persons when in conversation and/or conflict with others who hold non-affirming beliefs;

- Hosting discussions with transgender people about their needs, thoughts, and concerns, including medical care and costs; and

4. Cameron and Berkowitz, "The State of Gay Rights around the World."

- Developing a reconciling statement for public and private display.

In addition to creating awareness about public and private witness, becoming open and affirming may provide challenges to existing policies within the congregation, requiring significant discussion and revision by the leadership.

Policy and Leadership

To demonstrate a commitment to justice for LGBTQIA+ persons, congregations must examine their own policies and leadership. How are less-often heard voices in LGBTQIA+ communities included and given voice? Sexual orientation and gender identity don't exist in a vacuum. Of special emphasis is the need to explore intersectionality and the LGBTQIA+ community. Intersectionality refers to the many ways oppression is experienced in our world and the way in which this affects an individual who identifies as LGBTQIA+. For example,

> A gay man has to deal with homophobia. A black man has to deal with racism. But a black gay man will have to deal with homophobia *and* racism (often at the same time). It is often the case that he will face racism inside the LGBT community and homophobia in the black community. . . . Having an intersectional identity often generates a feeling that someone does not completely belong in one group or another, and can lead to isolation, depression and other mental health issues.[5]

Intersectional identities may include gender, race, sexual orientation, gender expression, aging, physical, mental and emotional challenges, poverty, nationality, ethnicity, religious belief and more.

As congregations participate in legislative initiatives and community discussions, these moments can become educational opportunities for creating awareness of intersectionality and other issues that LGBTQIA+ persons face. When considering their policy and leadership, congregations should be intentional about:

- Maintaining a visible presence of LGBTQIA+ leaders in worship;

- Reviewing the by-laws, leadership structure, physical plant, and budgeting to assure inclusion of the needs of LGBTQIA+ persons;

5. Equality Network, "What is Intersectionality?"

- Providing queer church employees the same benefits provided to straight employees;

- Providing gender-appropriate and unisex bathrooms;

- Developing a strategy for speaking publicly to issues of importance to LGBTQIA+ persons, such as discrimination, harassment, AIDS, homophobia, and trans-murder;

- Advocating for LGBTQIA+ persons, through community education and legislation; and

- Preparing a media policy.

For example, an intentional media policy would consider and plan ahead for: Who speaks on behalf of LGBTQIA+ concerns in the congregation? Are there congregants who are LGBTQIA+ or parents of LGBTQIA+ people that would be available for public comments?

Programming

What programming might build up the church, stimulating ministry for and with LGBTQIA+ people? How can existing programs and activities be adapted to become more open and welcoming? Consider how to:

- Identify and explore contemporary issues related to LGBTQIA+ persons and include these themes in worship;

- Supporting adoption and other parenting options for straight and gay couples;

- Care for and support parents and children of LGBTQIA+ persons;

- Pray for individuals while maintaining appropriate privacy;

- Provide support for elderly LGBTQIA+ persons who may be living alone or encountering life changes without a wide network of family or community support; and

- Examine intersectionality in all areas of programming.

Programming may include Bible studies, topical discussions, prayer groups, missional efforts, letter-writing campaigns, and more.

As denominations are struggling with decisions about how best to achieve an ethical and just polity that is LGBTQIA+ inclusive, open and affirming congregations need to ally with each other as they continue to learn and grow in their LGBTQIA+ outreach. The following appendices provide an introduction to many of the resources available.

Appendices

GLOSSARY[1]

asexuality. Experiencing little or no romantic, emotional, and/or sexual attraction or eroticism. Asexuality is different from celibacy, which is a decision not to engage in sexual behaviors with another person.

biological sex. The biological attributes such as anatomy, chromosomes, and hormones that inform whether a person is male, female, or intersex. Where sex refers to biology, gender refers to the cultural and social understandings that are layered on top of biology.

cisgender. A term that is becoming increasingly popular to describe people who are not trans or gender variant—in other words, those whose gender identities, presentations, and behavior "match" (according to the gender binary) the sex they were assigned at birth. Cis- is a prefix with roots that mean "on the same side"; trans and cis are neutral descriptors.

gender binary. A system of classifying sex and gender into two distinct and disconnected forms—male/man/masculine and female/woman/feminine—and assigning all bodies, identities, roles, and attributes to one side or the other.

gender expression. The ways in which a person manifests masculinity, femininity, both, or neither through appearance, behavior, dress, speech patterns, preferences, and more.

---

1. These definitions are adapted from several sources. Alford-Harkey and Haffner, *Bisexuality*; National Center for Transgender Equality, "Transgender Terminology"; and Unitarian Universalist Association, "Transgender 101."

gender identity. An individual's internal sense of being male, female, or something else. Since gender identity is internal, one's gender identity is not necessarily visible to others and is independent of one's sexual orientation.

heterosexism. Similar to racism or sexism, this term refers to the systemic privileging of heterosexuality over other sexual orientations, or to the assumption or assertion of heterosexuality as the preferred cultural norm.

heterosexuality. An enduring romantic, emotional, and/or sexual attraction toward people of another sex. The term "straight" is a common term used to refer to heterosexual people.

homosexuality. An enduring romantic, emotional, or sexual attraction toward people of the same sex or gender. The term "gay" can refer to homosexual women or men, while the term "lesbian" refers only to homosexual women.

intersectionality. The multiply-connected nature of social categorizations such as race, class, and gender as they apply to a given individual or group, creating overlapping and interdependent systems of discrimination or disadvantage. For example, the ways in which a lesbian, African-American woman may experience racial discrimination around white people and heterosexism within an African-American community.

intersex. A term used for people who are born with a reproductive or sexual anatomy and/or chromosome pattern that does not seem to fit typical definitions of male or female. Intersex conditions are also known as differences of sex development (DSD).

LGBTQIA+. Referring to lesbian, gay, bisexual, transgender, questioning, queer, intersexual, androgynous, asexual, and other (+) persons who do not conform to the gender binary. The "A" may also refer to cisgender and heterosexual allies.

queer. A term used to refer to lesbian, gay, bisexual, and often also transgender people. Some use queer as an alternative to "gay" in an effort to be more inclusive. Depending on the user, the term has either a derogatory or an affirming connotation, reclaiming a term that was once widely used in a negative way.

sexual orientation. The gendered pattern of a person's sexual attractions, or the gender of the people a person is attracted to. Gender and sexual orientation are often lumped together, despite being different, because of societal expectations around sex, gender, and expression. Everyone has a sexual orientation.

transgender (adj.). Describing a person whose gender identity, expression, or behavior is different from those typically associated with their assigned sex at birth. Transgender individuals can be lesbian, gay, bisexual, queer, straight, or any other sexual orientation.

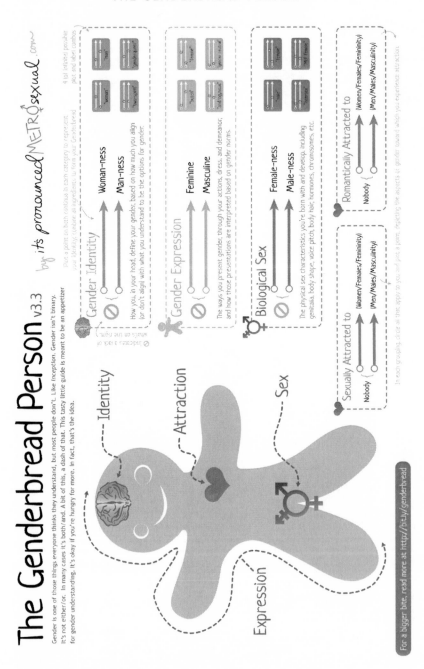

2. Killerman, "Breaking Through the Binary." Used with permission.

TEN IDEAS FOR BREAKING THE SILENCE AROUND SEXUALITY[3]

Being a welcoming and affirming congregation requires going beyond publicly proclaiming that "all are welcome." When lesbian, gay, bisexual, transgender, or queer (LGBTQ) people enter your faith community, will they actually experience welcome? Many congregations that profess to welcoming LGBTQ people don't talk much about LGBTQ issues or aren't prepared to address the needs of LGBTQ people in ministry. In part, that may because many faith communities are uncomfortable or under-educated about sexuality in general. Here are some ideas for breaking the silence around sexuality and around LGBTQ identities in your faith community.

- Talk with various groups in your faith community (e.g., parents, couples, LGBTQ people, young people) about sexuality programs they would like to be offered. Many denominations offer sexuality education resources, LGBTQ-specific resources, marriage and relationship enrichment programs, and support groups for congregants experiencing specific issues (adoptive parents, people with HIV, divorce groups, etc.). Create a team of clergy and lay people to develop a plan for moving the congregation forward.

- Ensure that clergy and staff have sexuality training that goes beyond abuse prevention and addresses sexual health, sexuality issues in ministry, and sexual justice concerns.

- Make an explicit statement—on your web site, in membership materials, on bulletin boards and other communications—that your faith community is welcoming and affirming to lesbian, gay, bisexual, transgender, and queer members. Read this statement aloud each week, saying each group individually. Share that clergy and staff are prepared to address sexuality issues in pastoral care with confidentiality and compassion.

- Preach a sermon or sermon series on sexuality, creation, and embodiment, or the role of women and LGBTQ people in your faith tradition.

- Observe important dates connected to sexuality issues—e.g., Transgender Visibility Day (March 31); National Teenage Pregnancy Prevention Month (May); LGBTQ Pride Month (June); National Coming

3. Provided by and published with permission of Drew Konow, Director of Communications and LGBTQ Programs at the Religious Institute.

Out Day (October 11); Transgender Day of Remembrance (November 20); or World AIDS Day (December 1), etc. Use sermons, prayers, and bulletin inserts to connect these events with faith.

- Lead a religious education session or Bible study on scriptural themes of sexuality, gender, marriage, love, and family.

- Convene an adult forum or study group on one or more sexuality issues being discussed in the news of the day, such as anti-LGBTQ bills, discrimination against transgender people in public accommodations, the recent murder of transgender women of color, the effects of affordable healthcare on LGBTQ communities, the impact of "defunding" Planned Parenthood on healthcare and sexuality education for LGBTQ people, etc. Invite a guest speaker or preacher to address these issues. If your denomination has published a statement or study on sexuality, this could be another springboard for discussion.

- Screen a feature film or documentary that deals with a contemporary sexuality issue—e.g., "Moonlight" and homosexuality, National Geographic's "Gender Revolution" and transgender identity, or "Juno" and teen pregnancy—and lead a group discussion.

- Host an open meeting for your congregants with leaders of a local LGBTQ advocacy organization or sexual and reproductive health agency, such as Planned Parenthood. Make pamphlets and other resources from these agencies available to your congregants, and ensure that clergy and staff have contacts for referrals.

- Add books on sexuality and religion to your library, and let congregants know they are there.

BECOMING A WELCOMING CONGREGATION

"A Welcoming Process is an officially recognized path that includes relational organizing, education, some kind of public vote and a public statement of Welcome for persons of ALL sexual orientations and gender identities."[4]

—Institute for Welcoming Resources

Open and affirming ministry requires years of preparation. Congregations often spend over a decade laying the groundwork before beginning an intentional process to become a Welcoming or Reconciling Congregation.[5] The Religious Institute offers the following guidelines:

"A typical process involves:

- Creating a team of clergy and lay persons (including both LGBT and non-LGBT persons) to begin the conversation and devise a plan for engaging the congregation.

- A self-assessment, such as a congregational survey or series of focus groups, to determine the congregation's needs.

- A time of sustained study, prayer and conversation, which may include youth and adult education, congregation-wide forums, study groups, sermon series, invited speakers and other activities.

- Developing a congregational statement of welcoming.

- A congregational vote.

Such a process may last anywhere from a period of months to two years or more."[6]

A Welcoming Process needs to be well-planned; informed by other congregations that have undergone a similar process; appropriate to the congregation's "personality"; based in relationship-building; and presented in the context of the ongoing ministry and mission of the congregation.[7]

---

4. Institute for Welcoming Resources, *Building an Inclusive Church*, 1.

5. RMN, *Reconciling Communities—How to get started!*. See also RMN, *Three Steps to Affiliate with Reconciling Ministries Network*.

6. Religious Institute, "Yes, We're Welcoming."

7. Institute for Welcoming Resources, *Building an Inclusive Church*, 1.

EIGHT PRINCIPLES OF HOLY CONFERENCING[8]

1. Every person is a child of God
2. Listen before speaking.
3. Strive to understand another's point of view.
4. Strive to reflect accurately the view of others.
5. Disagree without being disagreeable.
6. Speak about issues; do not defame people.
7. Pray, in silence or aloud before decisions.
8. Let prayer interrupt your busyness.

8. Dyck, *Eight Principles of Holy Conferencing.*

GROUP DISCUSSION QUESTIONS
Act I: Crying Out in New Birth

1. Consider how your personal story of origin shapes who you are today. How did you come to your faith? How did you come to the church?

2. Consider the faith stories of past generations of family members, friends, saints, communities, and congregations from which your faith emerges and in which your faith is grounded. Who are the Josephs that we may have forgotten?

3. How has a commitment to overcome social oppressions resulted in a "new birth" of awareness or experience for you or your faith community?

4. Consider a time in the life of your community or someone you love that required an act of "creative disobedience" in order to remain faithful. How has that act of faith shaped your understanding of what it means to be Christian?

5. When has your faith required you to stand against established powers, requiring you to act courageously—perhaps placing yourself at some risk?

6. Consider persons who played a role in conveying God's prevenient grace in your life. Who nurtured and protected you when you were most vulnerable? Who lifted you in an ark from the waters of uncertainty, social injustice, or spiritual infancy? Or, as Pastor Andrea asks: "Who or what is in your basket? Where is your Nile, and who, by God's grace, is standing on the other side of it, ready to take your hand?"

7. How has the study of scripture provided you with new meanings and insights at different stages of your life? What spiritual disciplines help you nurture the vision of faith so that it may grow in you as you mature in both years and faith?

8. Consider Mary Merriman's testimony in light of the theme "crying out in new birth." In her story, who cries out? Who experiences newness of life? When and where is God present?

Act II: Called Out to a New Role

1. Do you have a "called out" moment in your life? How have you experienced being called out by God at a particular time and place?

2. How has your faith community helped you to recognize, name, and call out injustices in the world today? Into what kind of mission and ministry has this developed in your congregation?

3. Where did you learn about sexuality when growing up? Who taught you about God's good gift and how to care for yourself and others as sexual beings? What did your church community teach you about sexuality, deliberately or inadvertently?

4. HIV/AIDS has been referred to as a plague. Where is God in this? What kind of theological attributions have you heard spoken (or shouted) about AIDS and God's intentions? Which arguments did you find helpful? Faithful? Hurtful?

5. We've met many modern-day characters so far in this book, including Cameron and her district superintendent, William Parker, Reverend Snyder, Adrian Cronauer's supervisor, Frank Schaefer, the Polk County Health Department director, Marie, Gail, and their physician, as well as the contributors of these stories. Who plays the role of Pharaoh? Moses? Jethro? The midwives? The Israelites? What parallels and differences do you see in the roles of modern-day persons and the characters of Exodus?

Act III: Coming Out with a New Identity

1. As the Israelites found themselves set apart from the Egyptians and led by Moses across the Sea of Reeds, how much choice do you think they had in this situation? Do you think that individuals today feel a similar degree of choice (or lack of) in "coming out" as gay, lesbian, transgender, or queer?

2. Try to remember times in your childhood or young adulthood in which you learned of the sexuality or sexual identity of others. How have these experiences shaped the way you understand LGBTQIA+ persons of faith?

3. Name some coming-out moments in your life or the lives of those you love. How have these moments shaped the relationships you now hold dear? How has your relationship with God changed or grown as a result?

4. Mary Merriman talks about all of the healing that needs to take place—individually, between persons, within communities, and in our relationships with God. How has your congregation helped you heal? How can your congregation become a more intentional place of healing and reconciliation for all persons?

5. What are the defining, coming-out moments for your congregation, when it realized or reaffirmed its identity as a faith community? How did this affect the vitality of worship, mission, and prayer in the congregation?

6. Why is it important for congregations to make public statements of welcome for LGBTQIA+ persons? Is a statement on the church website sufficient? Is it necessary to draw attention to being open and affirming, or can a congregation engage in this kind of ministry quietly? What is at stake, and what does this say about our faith in God?

7. Vision of Hope MCC overcame resistance in Mountville, in large part due to the concerted efforts of Mary and Dean to encourage discussion and relationship-building among the congregants in their respective congregations. How might this story embolden your congregation to become better allies to LGBTQIA+ persons?

Act IV: Figuring Out in a New Voice

1. How has your congregation navigated the sometimes-tumultuous social change in the society around it, particularly with regard to sexuality and gender?

2. How has the Holy Spirit disrupted your understanding of sexuality, gender, and church? For many of us, sexuality education in school and church did not include anything about intersex or transgender persons. Might openness to new scientific insights and to hearing from persons with different life experiences be considered a movement of the Spirit? How can we be open to what the Spirit is doing now or next?

3. Using the United Methodist guidelines about the church and the charismatic movement, in what ways can your congregation be open to and discerning of new *charisms* in its midst?

4. Figuring out how to respond to social change can seem a lot like wandering in the desert, thirsty and lost. What do your grumblings tell you about your hopes and fears during times of profound change?

5. If God can change, perhaps so can we. In the story of Exodus, the Hebrews' identity as the people of God is solidified only after the golden calf incident. What idols do we in the church need to abandon in order to live fully into our identity as disciples of Christ?

6. Consider the passage from John 6:25–35. Just as God gave the Israelites manna from heaven to eat, God provides "the bread from heaven" for us. What does it mean to you that Jesus claims to be "the bread of life"?

7. If "love trumps all," what does this mean for how we receive and carry on our religious traditions? In what ways does Jesus's priority of loving relationships over strict adherence to rules help us navigate social change? In what ways might it sow further confusion?

Act V: Setting Out on a New Journey

1. Michael Alleman offers something like a valedictory in his sermon "The View from Mount Nebo." As the pastoral leader of Grandview for twenty years, he casts a vision for a congregation that will set out on a journey without him as their leader. What questions does this raise about how we convey our hopes and dreams to the next generation and how we equip our children in the faith to navigate the social challenges that they will face in their lifetimes?

2. Open and affirming ministry is about removing barriers to the church's expression of God's love. It is ministry at the edges, and the edges are always changing. Where are the edges of your congregation's ministry today? What were they fifty years ago? What will they be fifty years from now?

3. What would have happened if Pilate had not washed his hands of responsibility, abdicating any power he might have had in the situation?

What responsibilities are we washing our hands of today? When have we refused to get involved or to exercise our power in Christ?

4. In the sermon "Responsibility / Refuge," what did you assume about the country of origin and political context of this refugee before realizing that the story was about Mary Merriman in Florida and Pennsylvania? How does this framing of Mary's struggle for civil rights change the way you think about the experiences of gay and lesbian people in the U.S.? Where do you find yourself in this story?

5. With a friend or prayer partner, read the lyrics to Marsha Stevens's song, "For Those Tears I Died." How does her response to the Good News of Jesus Christ resonate with your own experience? When in your life have you asked, "But Jesus, why me?"

6. The conversation of Grandview voices in Act V is wide-ranging and diverse, including cultural differences from the U.S., Africa, and Europe, as well as what the current, younger generation may be experiencing. Where is the hope in this conversation? Can history itself be a form of hope for the future?

7. Create a timeline of significant events in the life of your congregation. Share your own faith story in light of this timeline. Where has God acted in this history? Where is God leading you now?

Bibliography

Alexie, Sherman. *Indian Killer.* New York: Atlantic Monthly, 1996.

Alford-Harkey, Marie and Debra W. Haffner. *Bisexuality: Making the Invisible Visible in Faith Communities.* Westport, CT: Religious Institute, 2014.

AVERT. "History of HIV and AIDS Overview." http://www.avert.org/professionals/ history-hiv-aids/overview.

Bailey, Sarah Pulliam. "Ex-gay Group Exodus International Shuts Down, President Apologizes." *Religion News Service,* June 20, 2013. http://religionnews. com/2013/06/20/exodus-international-to-shut-down-after-presidents-apology-to-gay-community/.

Barker, Joel A. "The New Business of Paradigms." http://www.joelbarker.com/speeches/ the-power-of-paradigms/.

Borg, Marcus J. and John Dominic Crossan. *The Last Week: The Day-by-Day Account of Jesus's Final Week in Jerusalem.* San Francisco: HarperSanFrancisco, 2006.

Browning, Elizabeth Barrett. "Aurora Leigh." In *The Oxford Book of English Mystical Verse: XIII–XX Centuries.* Chosen by D. H. S. Nicholson and A. H. E. Lee. London: Clarendon, 1917.

Brueggemann, Walter. "Variations from the Barrio." In *The Collected Sermons of Walter Brueggemann,* with a preface by Samuel Wells, 263–71. Louisville: Westminster John Knox, 2011.

Cameron, Darla, and Bonnie Berkowitz. "The State of Gay Rights around the World." *Washington Post,* June 14, 2016. https://www.washingtonpost.com/graphics/world/ gay-rights/.

Crescente, Fernanda. "Clifton Church Vandalized with Sexual Slurs." Cincinnati.com, March 29, 2017. http://www.cincinnati.com/story/news/2017/03/29/clifton-church-vandalized-sexual-slurs/99791756/.

Crew, Louie. "Queer Eye for the Lectionary: Weekly Reflections on the Revised Common Lectionary by a Queer Episcopalian," August 24, 2008. http://queereye4lectionary. blogspot.com/2008/08/sunday-august-24th-2009.html.

De Gruchy, John W. *The Church Struggle in South Africa.* Eugene, OR: Wipf and Stock, 2000.

Dyck, Sally. *Eight Principles of Holy Conferencing: A Study Guide for Churches and Groups.* Minneapolis, 2012. http://mnumc-email.brtapp.com/files/eefiles/documents/holy_ conferencing_study_guide_2012.pdf.

Embrace. https://www.facebook.com/groups/embraceLanc/.

Equality Network. "What is Intersectionality?" http://www.equality-network. org/?s=racism.

Fox, Ruth. "Strange Omission of Key Women in the Lectionary," *National Catholic Reporter* 30.28 (May 13, 1994).

Fretheim, Terence E. *Exodus*. Interpretation. Louisville: John Knox, 1991.

"Fugitive Slave Act 1850." In The Avalon Project: Documents in Law, History and Diplomacy. Yale Law School. http://avalon.law.yale.edu/19th_century/fugitive.asp.

Grandview United Methodist Church. http://grandviewumc.org.

Hamilton, Adam. *Making Sense of the Bible: Rediscovering the Power of Scripture Today*. New York: HarperOne, 2014.

Harding, Vincent. *There is a River: the Black Struggle for Freedom in America*. New York: Harcourt Brace Jovanovich, 1981.

Hughes, Langston. "Freedom [1]." In *The Collected Poems of Langston Hughes*, edited by Arnold Rampersad with David Roessel. Vintage Classics. New York: Random House, 1994.

Institute for Welcoming Resources. *Building an Inclusive Church: A Welcoming Toolkit 2.0*. Washington, DC: National Gay and Lesbian Task Force, 2013. http://www. welcomingresources.org/welcoming.xml.

Jacobs, A. J. *The Year of Living Biblically: One Man's Humble Quest to Follow the Bible as Literally as Possible*. New York: Simon & Schuster, 2007.

Killerman, Sam. "Breaking Through the Binary: Gender Explained Using Continuums." http://itspronouncedmetrosexual.com/2011/11/breaking-through-the-binary-gender-explained-using-continuums/#sthash.RIEqYUqe.dpbs.

King, Martin Luther Jr., "I See the Promised Land." In *A Testament of Hope: The Essential Writings and Speeches of Martin Luther King, Jr.*, edited by James Melvin Washington, 279–86. San Francisco: HarperSanFrancisco, 1991.

Knotts, Alice G. *Fellowship of Love: Methodist Women Changing American Racial Attitudes, 1920–1968*. Nashville: Kingswood, 1996.

Maddox, Randy L. *Responsible Grace: John Wesley's Practical Theology*. Nashville: Abingdon, 1994.

Metropolitan Community Churches. "History of MCC." http://mccchurch.org/overview/history-of-mcc/.

Miller, Calvin. *The Singer Trilogy: The Mythic Retelling of the Story of the New Testament*. Downers Grove, IL: InterVarsity, 1990.

Murray, Peter C. *Methodists and the Crucible of Race 1930–1975*. Columbia, MO: University of Missouri Press, 2004.

National Center for Transgender Equality. "Transgender Terminology." January 15, 2014. http://www.transequality.org/issues/resources/transgender-terminology.

Pardes, Ilana. *Countertraditions in the Bible: A Feminist Approach*. Cambridge, MA: Harvard University Press, 1992.

PFLAG. https://www.pflag.org.

Presbyterian Church in Taiwan. "A Declaration on Human Rights." August 16, 1977. http://www.taiwandocuments.org/pcto4.htm.

Reconciling Ministries Network (RMN). *Reconciling Communities—How to get started!* http://www.rmnetwork.org/newrmn/wp-content/uploads/2014/10/RC-process-How-to-get-started1.pdf.

———. *Sample Reconciling Statements*. http://www.rmnetwork.org/newrmn/wp-content/uploads/2014/10/SampleReconcilingStatements.pdf.

———. *Three Steps to Affiliate with Reconciling Ministries Network.* http://www.rmnetwork.org/newrmn/wp-content/uploads/2014/10/RMN-Three-Steps-to-Affiliate-March2015.pdf.

———. "Vision." https://www.rmnetwork.org/newrmn/who-we-are/mission/.

Religious Institute. "Ten Ideas for Breaking the Silence Around Sexuality." Personal correspondence.

———. "Yes, We're Welcoming. Should We Make It Official?" http://religiousinstitute.org/acting-out-loud/yes-were-welcoming-should-we-make-it-official/.

Rios, Simón. "Anti-Semitic Taunts at a High School Basketball Game in Newton Spark Outrage." WBUR, March 14, 2016. http://www.wbur.org/morningedition/2016/03/14/catholic-memorial-newton-north-anti-semitic-taunts.

Roberts, Gary L. *Massacre at Sand Creek: How Methodists Were Involved in an American Tragedy.* Nashville: Abingdon, 2016.

Roosevelt, Theodore. "Citizenship in a Republic." Speech delivered at the Sorbonne, in Paris, France, April 23, 1910. http://www.theodore-roosevelt.com/trsorbonnespeech.html.

Schaefer, Franklyn. http://franklynschaefer.com.

Schneidau, Herbert N. *Sacred Discontent: The Bible and Western Tradition.* Baton Rouge: Louisiana State University Press, 1976.

Springsteen, Bruce. "O Mary Don't You Weep," 2005. https://www.youtube.com/watch?v=tebjshm7f_I.

Stephens, Darryl W. "A Charismatic Learning: Open and Affirming Ministry in a Methodist Congregation." *International Journal of Practical Theology* (forthcoming).

———. "In Landslide Vote, United Methodists Renew Resolve to be 'Open and Accepting.'" *United Methodist Insight,* June 29, 2016. http://um-insight.net/general-conference/2016-general-conference/part-1-in-landslide-vote-united-methodists-renew-resolve-to-/.

Stevens-Pino, Marsha. *For Those Tears I Died: The Amazing Story About How One Song Brought Healing to Millions and Birthed Contemporary Christian Music.* Reno, NV: Canyonwalker, 2016.

Travis, Stephen. *The Bible in Time: A Chronological Exploration of 130 Passages.* Nashville: Abingdon, 1997.

Unitarian Universalist Association. "Transgender 101: Identity, Inclusion, and Resources." http://www.uua.org/lgbtq/identity/transgender.

The United Methodist Church (UMC). *The Book of Discipline of The United Methodist Church 1972.* Nashville: United Methodist, 1972.

———. *The Book of Discipline of The United Methodist Church 2016.* Nashville: United Methodist, 2016.

———. "Guidelines: The UMC and the Charismatic Movement." In *The Book of Resolutions of The United Methodist Church 2016,* 683–96. Nashville: United Methodist, 2016.

United Methodist Women. "150th Anniversary of United Methodist Women." http://www.unitedmethodistwomen.org/150.

Williams, Michael E., ed. *The Storyteller's Companion to the Bible: Exodus–Joshua,* vol. 2. Nashville: Abingdon, 1992.

World Council of Churches. *Baptism, Eucharist, and Ministry.* https://www.oikoumene.org/en/resources/documents/commissions/faith-and-order/i-unity-the-church-and-its-mission/baptism-eucharist-and-ministry-faith-and-order-paper-no-111-the-lima-text.

Yrigoyen, Charles Jr. *John Wesley: Holiness of Heart & Life*, with study guide by Ruth A. Daugherty. Nashville: Abingdon, 1999.

ADDITIONAL SUGGESTED READINGS

Brownson, James V. *Bible, Gender, Sexuality: Reframing the Church's Debate on Same-Sex Relationships*. Grand Rapids: Eerdmans, 2013.

Brubaker, Ellen A. *The Bible and Human Sexuality: Claiming God's Good Gift*. Participant Guide by M. Garlinda Burton. New York: United Methodist Women, 2016.

Dant, Jim. *This I Know: A Simple Biblical Defense for LGBTQ Christians*. Macon, GA: Nurturing Faith Inc., 2018.

De la Torre, Miguel A. *A La Familia: A Conversation about Our Families, the Bible, Sexual Orientation and Gender Identity*. With Ignacio Castuera and Lisbeth Melendéz Rivera. The National Gay and Lesbian Task Force, the Human Rights Campaign Foundation and UNID@S. 2011. http://www.thetaskforce.org/static_html/downloads/release_materials/tf_a_la_familia.pdf.

Fishburn, Janet Forsythe, ed. *People of a Compassionate God: Creating Welcoming Congregations*. Nashville: Abingdon, 2003.

Gaede, Beth Ann, ed. *Congregations Talking about Homosexuality*. Herndon, VA: Alban, 1998.

Godsey, Heather, and Lara Blackwood Pickrel, eds. *Oh God, Oh God, Oh God! Young Adults Speak about Sexuality and Christian Spirituality*. St. Louis: Chalice, 2010.

Gushee, David P. *Changing Our Mind*, 2nd ed. Canton, MI: David Crumm, 2015.

Harbison, William L. and Phillip F. Cramer. *The Fight for Marriage: Church Conflicts and Courtroom Contests*. Nashville: Abingdon, 2018.

Human Rights Campaign Foundation. *A Christian Conversation Guide: Creating Safe and Inclusive Spaces for People Who are Lesbian, Gay, Bisexual & Transgender*. http://www.hrc.org/resources/a-christian-conversation-guide.

Knight, Henry H. III and Don E. Saliers. *The Conversation Matters: Why United Methodists Should Talk with One Another*. Nashville: Abingdon, 1999.

Martin, Colby. *Unclobber*. Louisville: Westminster John Knox, 2016.

McClintock, Karen A. *My Father's Closet*. Columbus, OH: Trillium, 2017.

Miller, Joe Jr. *Homosexuality: A Scriptural Way Forward for The United Methodist Church*. Gonzalez, FL: EnerPower Press, 2015.

Oliveto, Karen P. *Our Strangely Warmed Hearts: Coming Out into God's Call*. Nashville: Abingdon, 2018.

Oliveto, Karen P., Kelly D. Turney, and Traci C. West. *Talking About Homosexuality: A Congregational Resource*. Holy Conversations series. Cleveland, OH: Pilgrim, 2005.

Ott, Kate. *Sex + Faith: Talking with Your Child from Birth to Adolescence*. Louisville: Westminster John Knox, 2013.

Our Whole Lives. http://www.uuabookstore.org/cw_Search.aspx?k=our+whole+lives.

Reconciling Ministries Network. "Top 10 Reasons to Affiliate with Reconciling Ministries Network." http://www.rmnetwork.org/newrmn/wp-content/uploads/2014/10/RMN-Top-10-Reasons-to-Affiliate-with-RMN.pdf.

Religious Institute. "A Time To Seek: Study Guide on Sexual and Gender Diversity," http://religiousinstitute.org/timetoseek/.

———. "Acting Out Loud," http://religiousinstitute.org/acting-out-loud/.

Roller, Ermalou McDuffie. *On Thundering Wings: Homosexuality, Love, and the Church on Trial*. Winterset, IA: Golden Tree Communications, 2010.

Ruden, Sarah. *Paul Among the People*. New York: Pantheon, 2010.

Sledge, Robert W. "The Saddest Day: Gene Leggett and the Origins of the Incompatible Clause," *Methodist History* 55 no 3 (April 2017) 145–79.

Smith, Ted A., ed. *Frequently Asked Questions About Sexuality, the Bible, and the Church*. San Francisco: Covenant Network of Presbyterians, 2006.

Tigert, Leanne McCall and Timothy Brown, eds. *Coming Out Young and Faithful*. Cleveland: Pilgrim, 2001.

Voelkel, Rebecca. *To Do Justice: A Study of Welcoming Congregations*. Washington, DC: National Gay and Lesbian Task Force's Institute for Welcoming Resources, 2009. www.WelcomingResources.org.

Voelkel, Rebecca, et al. *Building an Inclusive Church: A Welcoming Toolkit 2.0*. Washington, DC: National Gay and Lesbian Task Force's Institute for Welcoming Resources, 2013. www.WelcomingResources.org.

Vrieze, Allan. *A Reconciling Cookbook: Recipes for an Inclusive Church*. Chicago: Reconciling Congregation Program, 1999.

Wallace, Catherine M. *Confronting Religious Denial of Gay Marriage: Christian Humanism and the Moral Imagination*. Eugene, OR: Cascade, 2015.

Wilson, Ken. *A Letter to My Congregation*. Canton, MI: Read the Spirit, 2014.

Wink, Walter, ed. *Homosexuality and Christian Faith: Questions of Conscience for the Churches*. Minneapolis: Fortress, 1999.

WEBSITES WITH ADDITIONAL RESOURCES

Believe Out Loud. http://believeoutloud.com/background/christianity-and-lgbt-equality.

Human Rights Campaign Foundation: http://www.hrc.org/resources/topic/religion-faith.

Institute for Welcoming Resources: http://www.welcomingresources.org/resources.htm and http://www.welcomingresources.org/links.htm.

Reconciling Ministries Network. https://www.rmnetwork.org/newrmn/resources-v2/.

Religious Institute. http://religiousinstitute.org/lgbt-equality/.

Made in United States
North Haven, CT
29 December 2021

13849723R00121